WORLD WAR TWO

TANKS

WORLD WAR TWO
TANKS

GEORGE FORTY

OSPREY
AUTOMOTIVE

Published in Great Britain in 1995 by Osprey,
Michelin House, 81 Fulham Road, London SW3 6RB

© 1995 The Book Package Company Limited.

Reprinted Summer 1996, Autumn 1998

ISBN 1 85532 532 2

Originated & produced by The Book Package Company Ltd.
Bournemouth, England.

Editor: Jasper Spencer-Smith

Design: John Clark, BA

Set in 10pt on 11.5pt Monotype Bembo.

Page make-up & Reprographics by

Appletone Graphics

Bournemouth, England

Printed in Hong Kong

ACKNOWLEDGMENTS

As always, I have many people to thank for their assistance with this book. First and foremost are those other authors who have generously allowed me to quote from their existing work or to use their photographs. Next I must thank David Fletcher, Librarian at the Tank Museum (TM) and his staff, in particular Roland Groom the resident photographer, for their invaluable help. Many of the photographs come from the Tank Museum collection, the rest are from other museums and private individuals and their names appear with their photographs. To all I extend my warmest thanks for their kind assistance, in particular to Judge Jim Osborne of the Indiana Military Museum, Vicennes, USA.

Lieutenant Colonel George Forty, OBE, FMA.

Bryantspuddle, March 1995

Title pages: Cruiser Tanks of 5RTR move forward to engage the enemy in France, May 1940. They are led by an up-armoured version of A 13, the A 13 Mk II or Cruiser Tank Mk IVA. Sadly all were knocked out or abandoned. (TM)

Turan I medium tank crosses a damaged bridge, watched by Hungarian soldiers - note their distinctive helmets. (TM)

CONTENTS

CHAPTER ONE

Great Britain

'Within the period of a generation, a time may come again when we shall have to defend our lives and our liberties. We lead the world in the design and manufacture of tanks. Let us not abandon that lead in the production of a vital weapon'.

Clough William Ellis, 1919.

For the nation that had invented the tank and had used it with increasing success in World War One, building over 3,000 heavy and medium tanks before hostilities ceased, Britain was in a desperately parlous state as far as its armoured forces were concerned when war in Europe once again became a reality. The last tank action of World War One had taken place on 5 November 1918, when eight Whippets of the 5th Battalion, Tank Corps, supported the 3rd Guards Brigade near the Mormal Forest. The armoured cars of the 17th Battalion, Tank Corps, had been in the vanguard of the final Allied advance which preceded the armistice of November 1918.

A staggering 2,000 plus tanks and armoured cars of the Tank Corps had been fighting almost non-stop for the last 100 days of the war, showing time and time again that the tank was a undoubtedly a battle winner. However, all this would not save the new weapon system from the prejudice which still pervaded the War Office. When the 'real soldiering' of peacetime put the beloved horse back on to its pedestal, then such dirty, smelly machines – battle winners though they might have been – could be safely relegated to the scrap heap. Besides, they were expensive to build and maintain, while the far flung outposts of the British Empire could be held in peacetime by small numbers of infantry, gunners and sappers, even if they did have to be supported from time to time by aircraft and armoured cars - at least they did not have those terribly noisy tracks or make such a muddy mess everywhere!

So the nation whose General Tank had, according to German historian A. W. H. von Zwehl, made a far greater contribution to victory than anything else, was about to reduce its eighteen tank battalions down to just four and to continue to threaten the security of this residue, until it finally received a degree of permenancy by obtaining Royal approval on 18 October 1923, when it became the Royal Tank Corps (RTC). The process of attrition and general War Office disinterest in tanks, however, continued, despite continual warnings from such 'gurus' of armoured warfare as Boney Fuller, the original architect of tank tactics. Nevertheless, mechanisation had to come in the end and with it came a hasty tank building programme. Sadly this was far from perfect not being helped by a number of bad policy decisions, one being that it was considered that three types of tanks were needed for the varying roles of armour on the battlefield. These were; firstly, the light, fast tanks for reconnaissance and scouting missions; medium /cruiser tanks which could also move about rapidly, yet supposedly possessed the firepower and protection to make their presence decisive in a battle; and finally, heavier but well-protected tanks, which could support infantry in both the assault and defence. The ideas that the reconnaissance tasks could be carried out by armoured cars and the other two roles by a single universal type of tank, did not find favour until the war was well in progress and the problems brought about by muddled pre-war thinking had come to the fore.

By 1938, with mechanisation in full swing even more light tanks were needed to replace horses in the newly mechanising cavalry units, which provided reconnaissance for the growing number of infantry divisions. Thus, there was an excess of light tanks, which did not matter in peacetime as they were cheap to build, easy to maintain and ideal for training. However, they would be rapidly outclassed on the battlefield when the shooting war began.

Even more damaging was the fact that, of the three basic tank characteristics namely firepower, protection and mobility, firepower was given the lowest priority in all three types of tank. Nowadays, the *raison d'etre* for a tank is to carry direct firepower about on the battlefield, but that was not the case in the 1930s. The British heavy tank of 1916-18 had had two 6 pounder guns as its main armament, capable of firing a mixture of armour piercing (AP), high explosive (HE) and cased shot (canister), together with four machine guns (MG) as its secondary armament. In World War Two, no tank in British Army service would be anywhere near as well equipped with such firepower, until the arrival (from the US) of the Lend-Lease M3 Grant medium tank in the Western Desert, 1942. Until that time the armoured regiments had to struggle along with tanks armed with either machine guns, or 2 pounders, which were quite good anti-tank weapons but useless for the support of infantry. Even when money became available and tank building became a priority, the British were still

bedevilled by too many different models, most of which had turret rings that were far too small to allow for larger guns to be fitted.

In 1936, the total strength of British tank forces amounted to just 375, of which 164 were obsolescent Vickers Mediums, whilst the rest were light tanks built since 1929 and armed only with machine guns. When war broke out in September 1939, there were 1,000 light tanks but only 146 of the new cruiser and infantry tanks. Nevertheless, production was increasing rapidly with more tanks being produced in Britain in 1939 than in Germany. The following year the output was almost equal - 1,399 in Britain as compared with 1,460 in Germany.

TANK PRODUCTION 1939-45

Year	Total	Comments
1939	969	In addition there were the pre-war models still in service
1940	1,399	Nearly 700 tanks were lost in France by the BEF
1941	4,841	From 1941, British armoured units were also increasingly equipped with American built tanks
1942	8,611	
1943	7,476	
1944	4,600	
1945	1,392	For the first six months only
TOTAL	29,288	

Above: **Churchill Mk VIs of 4th Battalion Grenadier Guards and accompanying infantry of 1st Battalion Suffolks advance through a Dutch village, 1944. Note the extra armoured protection by adding trackplates to the front glacis and turret.** *(TM)*

Above: **A Light Mk IIB (India pattern) on trials in India, 1935. These little tanks did extremely well, especially over the rough terrain of the North West Frontier. Note the square-shaped non-rotating cupola on top of the turret.** *(TM)*

Right: **Two Light Mk VIBs on the Bovington training area. The Mk VIB was the most widely used version during World War Two.** *(TM)*

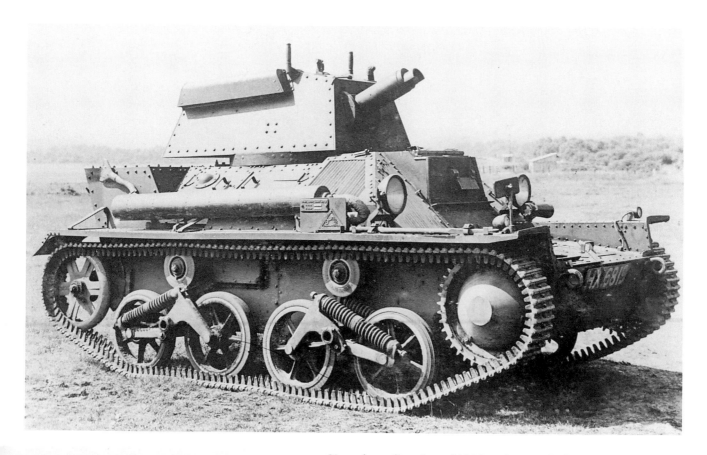

Since the earliest days of 1916, tank crews had named their vehicles and this custom continues, mainly now with special regimental names being used. However, the British also began in World War Two to officially name the types of tanks in service. This did not always happen, for example, the Light Mk VIB was never named, whereas both the Light Mk VII and Mk VIII were named (Tetrach and Harry Hopkins respectively), while the Infantry tanks Mk I & Mk II were both named Matilda. Sometime probably about mid-1940, the Cruiser Tank Mk V was officially given the name Covenanter, and the practice of using names beginning with the letter 'C' for main tank types carries on to the present.

Above: **The Light Mk III entered service in 1933 and was very similar to the MkII, except that the superstructure was extended at the rear.** *(TM)*

LIGHT TANKS

Although there must have been the odd Carden-Loyd and Morris-Martel one and two-man tankettes still in existence when the war began, it had been decided in the late 1920s that the armoured reconnaissance vehicles of the RTC, had to have a turret. This had led to the light tank Mk I, built by Vickers Armstrongs, entering service in 1930. Light tanks Mk II, IIA, IIB, III, IV, V, VI, VIA, VIB & VIC followed, all being very similar in construction, armament and performance. Most of the models saw action, during the early war years, although the Mk VIB was the main type to

be used in battle. Light and fast, these little tanks (Mk VI dimensions - length: 12ft 11½in, height: 7ft 3½in, width: 6ft 9in) were all mechanically successful, but their thin armour and poor armament made these tanks extremely vulnerable to enemy fire.

The Light Mk VIB was the most widely-used British light tank of the war. Some 550 Light Mk VIs went to France, all but six were lost either in action or abandoned when the British Expeditionary Forces (BEF) had to withdraw. Winston Churchill stated in the House of Commons on 4 June 1940, 'The best of all we had to give had gone to the BEF, and although they had not the numbers of tanks and some articles of equipment which were desirable, they were a very well and fully equipped Army.' This army and those of its European allies had been thrashed by the Blitzkrieg tactics of the German Panzerwaffe.

The Light Mk VIs, especially the Mk VIBs, fought on in the Western Desert up to 1942, but were often outclassed finding themselves inevitably used against more powerful opposition. In the first seige of Tobruk, for example, 1st Royal Tank Regiment (RTR) used their sixteen light tanks to distract the German armour and to make them believe that the garrison was stronger than

was actually the case. Light Mk VIs also saw service in Greece, Crete and Malta (used for clearing airfield runways), while the Australians used them in Syria 1941.

This was not the end of the light tank line, two further models appeared – one prewar designed in 1936 and produced in 1940; the other designed during the war (1941) which never reached full production. The first, the Light Mk VII (A17), sometimes known by its code-name Purdah or PR tank which later (in 1943) became known as the Tetrach, was designed and built as a private venture by Vickers Armstrongs. It weighed 7.5 tons, had armour up to 16mm thick, a road speed of 37mph, a crew of three and mounted a 2 pounder gun as its main armament, together with a co-ax 7.92mm BESA machine gun. The coaxially mounted machine gun (co-ax) was fitted to the same mounting as the main gun, traversing and elevating with it; using the same controls and sights (although they had separate graticule patterns). A close support variant was armed with a 3 inch howitzer.

Vickers had intended the Mk VII to be used as a Cavalry Tank, which meant it had to be suitable for such roles as reconnaissance both close and distant; convoy and escort protection; covering

Below: **Light Mk VIBs being refurbished at the Abingdon Machine Gun Works, near Oxford, England.** *(TM)*

LIGHT TANKS Mark II to VI

Type	Date of design	Weight tons	speed mph	Armour mm	Armament MGs	Crew	Use
II, IIA & IIB	1929	4.5	30	4-10mm	one .303	two	GB – training

(some IIA & IIB were still in service in Middle East (ME) in 1940, with the Western Desert Force.)

Type	Date of design	Weight tons	speed mph	Armour mm	Armament MGs	Crew	Use
III	1933	4.5	30	12mm	one .303 or one .50	two	GB – training

(some were in service with a South African unit during the Abyssinian campaign of 1941.)

Type	Date of design	Weight tons	speed mph	Armour mm	Armament MGs	Crew	Use
IV	1934	4.5	36	12mm	as for Mk III	two	GB & overseas – training
V	1935	4.75	32.5	12mm	one .50 MG & one .303	three	as above

(A small number were used for trials with AA mounts - twin 15mm BESA MGs or a quadruple Browning aircraft turret - never used in action.)

Type	Date of design	Weight tons	speed mph	Armour mm	Armament MGs	Crew	Use
VI, VIA VIB & VIC	1935	5	35	4-14mm or 15mm	one .50 co-ax MG & one .303 or 7.92mm	three	GB then with BEF. Also in M E. Later used for training when replaced by other types (US Honeys).

(Some were used for mounting AA turrets with quadruple 7.92mm BESA MGs.)

force and flank protection; raids and acting as a mobile reserve.

What made this little tank (length: 13ft 6ins, height: 6ft 11½ins, width: 7ft 7ins) so different to its predecessors was its novel method of skid steering, designed by Leslie Little, which involved pivoting the wheels making the tracks bow and flex. A protoype was produced in 1937, but the Mk VII was not put into full production until 1940. A total of 177 only were built, some being immediately issued to armoured regiments in Great Britain due to the severe shortage of cruiser tanks. Later the Tetrach did see action, some being used on 6 June 1944 by airborne forces during the Normandy landings. They were ferried across to France in Hamilcar gliders, which had been specially designed to carry a single Tetrach. All were crewed by troops of the Airborne Armoured Reconnaissance Regiment. Prior to this operation, a few had been sent to Soviet Union for use by the Red Army. One British squadron equipped with this tank took part in the invasion of Madagascar in May 1942.

The Light Mk VIII (A25), originally described as a small cruiser tank was known as Harry Hopkins. It was a development of the Tetrach aimed at modernising and up-armouring its predecessor and used the same track-flexing steering, but with the addition of hydraulic-assisted controls for the driver. Vickers Armstrongs designed it in 1941 and, after the prototype had

been accepted, Metropolitan-Cammell Carriage Wagon Co Ltd built 92 in the period up to 1944. However, it did not enter service as a gun tank because there were enough Tetrachs and American-built Locusts (see Chapter 4) for the airborne role. Instead, some of the 8.5 ton A25s were converted into the Alecto SP (with either 95mm howitzer or 6 pounder gun), whilst others were completed as Alecto dozers. Another variant was the C26, an armoured personnel carrier (APC). As the end of the war came before the development phase was properly completed, the project was cancelled.

Finally, although the Vickers 6-ton tank was a private venture vehicle and never actually ordered by the British Army, some export models were taken over when war broke out and used for training. Initially there had been two models of this tank when it first appeared in 1928, the Type A with two separate fully traversing turrets, both mounting machine guns and the Type B with a single larger turret mounting a 47mm gun and a co-ax MG. In the 1930s they were purchased by Bolivia, Bulgaria, China, Finland, Greece, Poland, Russia and Thailand, forming the basis of their tank armies. Many were used in battle, for example, in Poland against the Germans; in China against the Japanese. Both sides in the Winter War between Russia and Finland deployed this tank. The Red Army also used the design to develop their T-26, while both Poland and USA produced very similar vehicles.

Medium Cruiser Tanks

There were still a number of these obsolescent medium tanks (Mks II, IIA, II★ & II★★) still in service at the start of the war, both in Britain and the Middle East, because this tank had been the standard equipment of the RTC throughout the 1920s and 1930s until the arrival of the cruisers and infantry tanks. Possibly a few even saw action with the Western Desert Force in 1940-41. Weighing 13.45 tons, with armour 8mm thick, the five-man Mk II was armed with a 3 pounder, plus three .303 Vickers MGs, top speed of 18mph and powered by a 90hp Armstrong Siddeley petrol engine. Vickers Armstrongs, to whom Britain owed so much for their solitary pioneering in between the wars, designed and built this tank.

The Cruiser Tank Mk I (A9) was designed, in early 1934 by Sir John Carden of Vickers Armstrongs, originally as a close support tank, mounting a 3.7inch mortar (Mk I CS) to complement the mediums, but finally became a replacement. It weighed 12 tons, was 19ft long, 8ft 2½ ins wide and 8ft 8½ins high, had armour 6-14mm thick, armed with a 2 pounder gun and three MGs - one co-ax and two in separate one-man turrets. Because

Left: **Last of the Light Mk VI was the Mk VIC, which had the Vickers machine guns replaced by 7.92mm and 15mm BESA machine guns. It also had broader tracks and wider supension wheels. These tanks were photographed somewhere (locations were kept secret) in England on aerodrome defence duty, 1941.** *(TM)*

Left: **A Tetrach (Light tank Mk VII) is loaded into a Hamilcar glider, which was specially designed and built to carry the 7.5 ton tank.** *(TM)*

of this armament it carried a crew of six. Powered by a six-cylinder 150hp AEC A179 petrol engine, the A9 had a top speed of 25mph and a radius of action of 100 miles. A total of 125 were built (only 50 by Vickers the rest by Harland & Wolff). A few A9s served in 1st Armoured Division with the BEF and later with 7th Armoured Division in North Africa, where they did well against the Italians. When the Afrika Korps arrived in 1941 they were soon outclassed by the German Panzers.

The Cruiser Tank Mk II (A10) again designed in 1934 by Sir John Carden, was originally intended as the more heavily armoured, infantry support version of the A9. Weighing 13.75tons, with armour 6-30mm thick, it closely resembled the A9, except that it was eight inches shorter and the twin one-man MG turrets were replaced by a single MG, reducing the crew to five men. In the Mk II, the turret MG was still a Vickers (co-axial to the 2 pounder), but the hull MG was now a 7.92mm BESA - making it the first British tank to be fitted with an air-cooled MG, while the Mk IIA also had a co-ax BESA. As with the A9 there was in addition a Mk IIA CS, equipped with a 3.7-inch howitzer. A total of 175, A10s were built (mainly Mk IIA), thirty-one going to France with the BEF while others saw action in the Western Desert alongside A9s. The A10 was classified as a Heavy Cruiser, however, after its performance in France the War Office reported that it was: 'underpowered, gave a very bad cross-country performance and was very slow.' This was hardly surprising as it was powered by the same engine as the lighter A9.

Far left: **An A10 (Cruiser Mk IIA) being loaded onto a tank transporter from an RAOC recovery unit.** *(TM)*

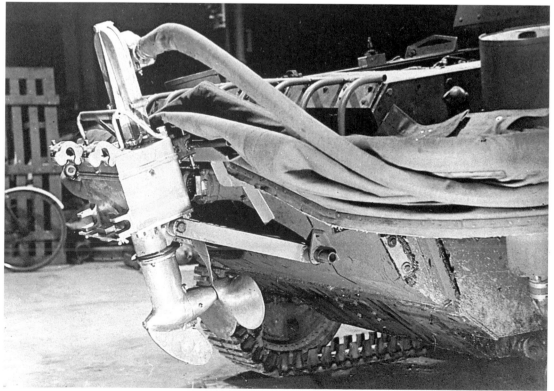

Left: **DD (Duplex Drive) propellor unit as trialled on Tetrach, this was the first of Straussler's innovative designs and was the test bed for later development.** *(TM)*

Above: **Last of the light tanks - the Light Mk VIII, Harry Hopkins. It was not used on active service, except as the Alecto dozer, there being enough Tetrachs and Locusts for use by the airborne forces.** *(TM)*

Right: **A9 (Cruiser Mk I) - this is in fact the close support version (Mk ICS), mounting a 3.7in howitzer instead of the normal 2 pounder gun. Note the two small machine gun turrets either side of the driver's station.** *(TM)*

Sir Noel Birch of Vickers reported to his fellow directors, after speaking with Major General Sir Hugh Elles in 1936 (when the latter was Master General of Ordnance and adamant that Vickers should have some competition in tank building) –'Elles has arranged with Nuffield to get a Christie tank over from America, the latest, which is supposed to have done so well in Russia.' This directly led to the long run of British cruiser tanks with Christie suspension.

J Walter Christie, an irascible but brilliant American engineer, was the designer of a revolu-

tionary new suspension system, which incorporated large road wheels and was capable of achieving high speeds both on roads and cross-country. Two vehicles with Christie suspension were purchased, shipped to Britain and work commenced on building prototype models at Morris Commercial Ltd. The first production models of the new tank, known as the A13, Cruiser Tank Mk III, emerged in 1939. Weighing 14 tons and powered by a V-12 340hp Nuffield Liberty petrol engine, the tank had a top speed of 30mph - nearly twice as fast as the A10. It was just over 19ft long,

7ft 4ins high and 8ft 6 ½ins wide. The tank's armour was still only the same thickness as that of the A9. The turret was similar in size and shape to that of the A9, except for a large commander's cupola, and carried the same gun. The initial order was for sixty-five and they saw service with the BEF and later with the 7th Armoured Division in the Western Desert.

The A13 Mk II or Cruiser Tank Mk IV was essentially an up-armoured version of the A13, with armour now up to 30mm thick (as required in the 1939 General Staff specification for armour thickness on all cruiser tanks). This was achieved by adding armour to the nose, glacis and turret front plus spaced armour on the turret sides. The extra armour added about a ton to its weight, but did not unduly affect overall performance. Also produced was a Mk IVA version with a BESA replacing the Vickers as MG co-ax armament.

Third of the A13s was the Mk III or cruiser tank Mk V, the ill-starred Covenanter, which differed in most respects to its predecessors. It had sleek good looks, a low silhouette (over 12 inches lower than the Mk II or III) and was powered by a flat-twelve 280hp Meadows engine, which allowed the 18-ton tank a top speed of 31mph. Unfortunately it broke down constantly, even when a new cooling system was designed it was still prone to overheating. Over 1700 were built, but the Covenanter was never judged good enough for operational service, and was only used for training. However, probably the greatest disservice done by Covenanter was the fact that they clogged up the production lines preventing the manufacture of improved tanks. A number of Covenanter tanks were fitted with the 34ft long and 9ft 6ins wide scissors-type bridge, a few of

Right: **Cruiser Mk IVA, last of the A13 types, shown on a driver training exercise in Britain.** *(TM)*

Right: **Moving a Crusader across a river by pontoon raft, during training exercises in Britain.** *(TM)*

Below: **A Covenanter bridgelayer launching its 30ft folding bridge. They were used mainly for training and development work, but a few were used by the Australians in Burma, 1942.** *(TM)*

which were used in the Far East by the Australians. There was also a trials installation of the Anti-Mine Roller Attachment (AMRA) in 1942.

Probably most famous of the early wartime cruisers was Crusader undoubtedly a better tank than Covenanter, although it also had many early teething troubles. A total of 5,300 were built between 1940 and 1943, by Nuffields and numerous other companies. The 19-ton tank initially had a crew of five – a commander, gunner, loader, driver and hull gunner, however, when the sub-turret was abandoned (on the recommendations of the Gunnery School) the crew was reduced to four. Then, when the tank was up-gunned from 2 pounder to 6 pounder (Crusader III), there was no room in the turret for the loader. The space which had been occupied by the sub-turret was also taken up by extra ammunition stowage. The tank was 19ft 8ins long, 7ft 4ins high and 8ft 8ins wide. Crusader first saw action in the Western Desert, June 1941. It was a popular tank, but no match for the German PzKpfw III or IV.

There were a number of adaptations of Crusader, including a number of anti-aircraft (AA) versions, observation post (OP), command,

armoured recovery vehicle (ARV), dozer, dozer and crane, gun tractor and Crusader with AMRA.

Crusader III - AA		
Mk	Type gun	Remarks
I	single 40mm Bofors	Turret removed, all round open – topped shield fitted
II	twin 20mm Oerlikon	Turret removed, new enclosed turret fitted
III	as for Mk II, but with radio in hull next to driver	

A fourth type with a triple 20mm Oerlikon in an open mount was also produced.

Above: **Despite its good looks, Covenanter was a disappointing tank and never saw active service, although over 1,700 were built. This is a pilot model, lacking the cast mantlet cover. The crew wear the early style crash helmets, made of thin, pressed and riveted fibre material.** *(TM)*

Above left: **This Crusader has been fitted with painted hessian screens so that it looks like a truck. This type was known as Houseboat, while the desert equivalent was Sunshade.** *(TM)*

Far right: **Cruiser Mk VIII (A 27L) Centaur, its main armanent was a 6 pounder gun, with two BESA machine guns (one co-ax and one hull mounted).** *(TM)*

Right: **Standard production Cruiser Mk VI (A 15) Crusader I, which came from the same line of development as Covenanter but was a far more reliable tank.** *(TM)*

The AA models were designed and produced for the Normandy invasion, a troop of AA tanks being allocated to most tank squadrons. However, when it became obvious that the Allies had total air superiority they were disbanded.

A new breed of Christie-type suspension cruiser tanks were designed from 1941 onwards, incorporating changes from lessons learnt in France and in the early operations of the Western Desert, together with crew experience from both

Above: **A Crusader dozer as used by the Royal Engineers. The turret was removed and a winch and jib fitted for its dozer blade.** *(TM)*

Right: **The 40 ton A33 heavy assault tank, was based upon Cromwell, but did not enter production as by 1943, the Churchill had proved itself, and the project was scrapped.** *(TM)*

Below: **A Cruiser Mk VIII (A 27L) Centaur. This is the Centaur IV 95mm howitzer version, from H Troop, 2nd Battery, 1 Royal Marine Armoured Support Regiment, here moving forward off the Normandy beaches, 1944.** *(TM)*

Covenanter and Crusader. First of these was Cruiser Tank Mk VII (A24) Cavalier, based on the Crusader III, but with thicker armour (up to 76mm) and wider tracks. The tank was 5 tons heavier but 5 mph slower as the engine and drive train remained unchanged. Cavalier was only produced in small numbers, some of which saw service as OP tanks.

It was followed immediately into service by the Cruiser Tank Mk VIII (A27L) Centaur with a 6 pounder gun (Mk I), the first production tanks being delivered in the late autumn of 1942. It had been intended to fit the V-12 600hp Rolls-Royce Meteor engine (a modified Merlin aero engine), but because of demand for the RAF the old V-12 Liberty engine was retained. However, it was mated to the new Merrit-Brown transmission enabling the 26-ton tank to achieve a top speed of 24mph. Most were used for training, but ninety Mark IVs (close support model with 95mm howitzer and an uprated engine) saw service in France, after the Normandy landings. Some Centaurs were converted to the AA role but most of the remainder were, in 1943, mod-

ified into Cromwells with the installation of the Rolls-Royce Meteor engine.

Centaur variants

AA MK I	-	with twin Polsten guns in mounting as for Crusader AA MkII
AA Mk II	-	as for Crusader AA Mk III but with twin Polsten guns
ARV	-	carried a demountable A-frame jib
Dozer	-	allocated to Cromwell equipped tanks squadrons
Kangaroo	-	without turret for use as APC
OP	-	with dummy gun and extra radios for artillery spotting

The fastest (up to 40mph) and most important of this trio of cruisers was Cruiser Tank Mk VIII (A27M) Cromwell, the first British tank to be originally designed with an all-welded hull (later models) and a V-12 600hp Rolls-Royce Meteor engine. It was 20ft 10ins long, 8ft 2ins high and 9ft 6 1/2ins wide. In 1944-45 it became the main equipment of many British armoured divisions, replacing the

Below: **A Centaur AA Mk II, mounted 20mm Polsten cannons on a Centaur III or IV chassis. A similar mounting was tried on the Crusader, but with twin Oerlikon cannons.** *(TM)*

Above: **A Cromwell ARV from 11th Armoured Division, towing a captured late model PzKpfw IV. Note the spaced armour around its turret to protect from Bazooka-type projectiles.** *(TM)*

Right: **Queen of the Desert, the A12 Matilda Mk II was greatly loved by its crews and was far superior to any Italian tank. It was outclassed by German PzKpfw III and IV.** *(TM)*

Top: **A Centaur ARV with the jib erected.** *(TM)*

Above: **A Centaur dozer at work.** *(TM)*

Shermans in those units destined to fight in north-west Europe. This was not always considered to be a fair exchange by many tank crews. For example, from the veteran 7th Armoured Division (the Desert Rats) which had been brought back from Italy by General Montgomery, especially for the invasion, one driver told the author: 'It was fast, reliable and good to drive, but for its intended role it was a disaster...' In March 1944, all drivers of the three regiments of 22 Armoured Brigade were sent to the Surrey test track of FVPE. To quote one driver : 'We did three weeks of road and cross-country tests with the Cromwells. At the end of the tests we were assembled in a hall before the top brass and asked for our opinion of the Cromwell. We told the truth which was almost unprintable!'

The major problem with the Cromwell was its lack of firepower in the tank versus tank situation, followed closely by lack of armoured protection, although this was addressed by the addition of applique armour, bringing its maximum thickness up to 101mm (normal 76mm). When the main tank battles of Normandy were over and the Germans were forced by heavy tank losses (which

were not made up), to rely on towed anti-tank guns. The Cromwell, with its 75mm gun, dealt effectively with these soft-skinned targets.

Mk of Cromwell	Main alterations
Mk I	6-pounder gun and two BESA MG
Mk II	no hull MG
Mk III	Centaur I re-engined (also known as Cromwell X)
Mk IV	Centaur II re-engined and with 75mm gun
Mk IVw	as for Mk IV, but with all-welded hull and R.R. Meteor engine
Mk Vw	all-welded hull
Mk VI	as for Mk IV with 95mm howitzer
Mk VII	re-worked MkIV with additional armour and wider tracks, speed governed to 32mph, 75mm gun
Mk VIII	re-worked Mk VI with 95mm howitzer and also ARV, Command/OP, mine exploder with CIRD

Right: **Cromwells on a training exercise in Britain. The leading tank is a Mk VI mounting a 95mm howitzer.** *(TM)*

Finally, mention must be made of the heavy assault tank the A33 which was produced (two pilot models only) in 1943 and based on the Cromwell hull and turret, but with added armour. Like the assault 'Jumbo' Sherman (see page 139), this tank came into being largely as a result of the bitter experience gained fighting against German armour in the Western Desert.

The Churchill (see page 49) was still having major development problems and it was felt that more could be gained by producing a universal chassis which could be used for both the cruiser and infantry tank. Such a tank needed to have adequate speed and reliabilty, good firepower and protection, thus, a heavier version of the Cromwell should be suitable for both roles. By using a common chassis, component production could be streamlined rather than producing a wide range of components for the then many types of obsolescent, unbattleworthy tanks.

Various design studies based on Cromwell were undertaken (A31 & A32), but the A33 was the only one to reach pilot production stage. At over 40 tons with armour up to 115mm thick, a top speed of 25mph and armed with the dual purpose 75mm gun, it sounded ideal. Unfortunately, the Christie-type suspension was unsuitable for the extra weight so the American-designed Horstmann suspension was fitted. The pilot A33s were produced in 1943, about the same time as Churchill proved itself in Tunisia, so the project was scrapped.

It had become clear from the tank battles in the Western Desert, that the British needed to produce a tank mounting a high velocity gun capable of knocking out all known German tanks. Initially it was proposed to mount the 3 inch AA gun on a Churchill, but this project was abandoned in favour of the newly developed 17 pounder gun. The Cromwell chassis had to be enlarged to make it capable of carrying a four-man turret large enough to carry the new gun and the extra loader. This was achieved in the A30 Challenger, based on Cromwell components but with a widened centre hull it was nearly six feet longer, and required an extra road-wheel to carry the additional weight. An order for 200 was placed and production began in December 1943, but by the end of September 1944 a total of only thirty-six had been produced (twelve for each of three armoured regiments).

Later in 1944, Challengers were delivered to armoured reconnaissance regiments to strengthen their firepower. Fortunately, as will be explained later, it had also been found possible to fit the 17 pounder into the M4 Sherman medium tank (then called Firefly), which was already in service with many British armoured regiments. Other drawbacks with the Challenger were; its very high silhouette - just under 12 inches higher than Cromwell; small amount of ammunition carried (42 rounds as

Above: **The A34 Comet was undoubtedly the best all-round British tank of the war but did not enter service until March 1945, so had little or no impact in the final World War Two tank battles.** *(GF)*

Right: **The A41 Centurion Mk I was the first of a highly successful line of medium gun tanks which continued for over 25 years. Armament is a 17 pounder gun and a 20mm Polsten cannon (only fitted to pilot models, later a co-ax BESA MG was fitted).** *(TM)*

opposed to 64 rounds for the Cromwell 6 pounder and 75mm, or 78 rounds for the Sherman Firefly); reduction in armour thickness everywhere except on the front of the turret.

It is a damning indictment of the shortcomings of British wartime tank design, that it took until the end of 1944 to bring into service a tank that was comparable in firepower, protection and mobility with the German Panther which had entered service two years earlier. Nevertheless, the A34 Comet was certainly well worth waiting for and it can be justifiably classed as the best British all-round tank of World War Two, although it did not arrive with operational units, in any large numbers, until after the Rhine crossing in March 1945. Comet mounted a 76.2mm (usually called a 77mm) Ordnance Quick Firing (OQF) gun as its main armament, which was capable of penetrating 130mm of homogeneous armour at 30 degrees from 2000 metres range using Armour Piercing Discarding Sabot (APDS) ammunition. The tank was of all-welded construction, with armour from 14-101mm thick and had a five-man crew (the fifth, a co-driver also manned a second BESA MG). The A34 was 25ft 1½ins long, 10ft wide and 8ft 9½ins high, with a maximum speed of 29mph and a radius of action of 123 miles. The tank remained in service with the British Army until 1960.

Top: **The 13.5 ton Vickers Medium Mk II* was the standard tank of the prewar RTC.** *(TM)*

Above: **The Vickers Light Mk VIB was the most widely-used British Light Tank of the war.** *(TM)*

Left: **Matilda Mk1 (All) Infantry Tank, had armour up to 60mm thick and was armed with machine guns.** *(TM)*

Right: **"Queen of the Desert", Infantry Tank (A12), Matilda Mk II. This fully restored example is painted to represent Golden Miller, the tank Lt. Col (later Major General) Bob Foote, DSO was commanding when as CO of 7 RTR, he won the Victoria Cross in the desert in 1942.** *(TM)*

Above: **Cruiser Tank Mark V, the Covenanter (A13 Mk III),** was a good looking tank with a low silhouette but was a poor performer, being only ever used for training. *(TM)*

Left: **Cruiser Tank Mk VI Crusader (A15) ,** was the best of the early wartime British cruisers. This version mounts a 6 pounder gun instead of the original 2 pounder. *(TM)*

Right: **Cruiser Tank Mk VIII, Cromwell (A27M) was light, fast and well armed with a 75 mm gun. British units brought back from the Middle East for D-Day, such as 7th Armoured Division, did not immediately like them, preferring their old Shermans.** *(TM)*

Left: **The Infantry Tank Mk IV was named the Churchill after the great wartime Prime Minister Winston Churchill. There were eleven Marks of Churchill, the Mk I mounted a 2 pounder gun in the turret and 3 inch howitzer in the hull. From Mk III onwards it was armed with a 6 pounder and from Mk VIII with a 75 mm gun.** *(TM)*

Below: **The Light Tank Mk VII, Tetrach was designed in 1936 but did not enter service until 1940. It saw action with British airborne forces during the Normandy landings, 6 June 1944.** *(TM)*

Above: **Infantry Tank Mk III, Valentine, was well liked by its crews and eleven different Marks were built, also numerous adaptations such as the SP guns Bishop and Archer.** *(TM)*

Right: **Best of the British Cruiser Tanks of World War Two, the A34 Comet. It continued in service after the war until replaced by Centurion in 1960. The 76.2mm gun had a performance comparable with that of the heavier German tanks.** *(TM)*

Although it was called a Heavy Cruiser when it was first mooted in August 1943, A41 Centurion was really the first of the current line of main battle tanks which could comfortably manage all the tasks given to armour, except perhaps that of stealthy reconnaissance. It did not fight in World War Two, although six Centurions Mk Is were delivered in May 1945 and rushed over to Germany for troop trials, but did not arrive until after VE-Day. Although it deserves a mention, it really played no part whatsoever in the war. Had it done so, then it would certainly have been a match for Tiger.

Infantry Tanks

The third major type of tank to see service in World War Two was the so-called Infantry Tank, designed to support infantry with protection as its main characteristic. These tanks would expect to come under heavy rifle and machine gun fire so splash-proofing was essential. This was a problem encountered in World War One with the thinly armoured heavy tanks, where there had been the injuries to tank crews caused by spawl (flakes of metal coming off the inside of the armour plate when struck on the outside by enemy fire) and splash (actual bullets or fragments entering through gaps/joints in the armour).

Speed did not matter as the tank would be moving at the same pace as infantry whilst its fire-power was initially, hardly considered as being very important. Two types were discussed; one small and inconspicuous, well protected but mounting only a machine gun; the other was larger, equally well protected and slow, but equipped with the basic anti-tank weapon (2 pounder OQF) to deal with enemy tanks but useless for infantry support. The other constraint that was placed from the outset of the design, in the

Above: **Infantry Tank Mk I (A11), the Matilda I, was a tough 11 tonner that travelled along at 8mph. These A 11s belonging to 4 RTR are in a French farmyard, 1940, as the crews prepare for battle.** *(GF)*

Right: **Heaviest armed of the Cruiser Tanks was A30 Challenger, which mounted a 17-pounder gun in a very tall, ungainly looking turret. The Sherman Firefly proved a better tank, so Challenger was not widely used.** *(GF)*

mid-1930s, was that it had to be inexpensive. The Infantry Tank A11, known also as the Matilda I (supposedly named after a cartoon duck who waddled along) matched all the criteria. It weighed 11 tons, was under 16ft long and just over 6ft high, had a crew of two was armed only with a single .5 or .303 machine gun had armour 10-60mm thick and a top speed of 8mph (3 to 4mph cross-country). Vickers built only 139 (plus the pilot model) and a number went to France with 4th and 7th RTR together with some Matilda Mk IIs. All took part in the famous Arras counter-attack, when for the very first time the all-conquering Panzerwaffe discovered that here were tanks which they could not easily knockout. The historian, Sir Basil Liddell-Hart, described Arras as being the battle which saved the BEF from complete destruction. Sadly, the Matilda lacked the ammunition and reserves necessary to do more than impose a short delay on the enemy. All were eventually lost. This was the one and only time the Mk Is were used in action, all being later relegated to the training role.

The Infantry Tank Mk II (A12), Matilda Mk II, was a vast improvement over its predecessor and, by mid-1941, had earned itself the title: 'Queen of the Desert' against the Italians but rapidly lost its popularity when German medium tanks and the 88mm FlaK (*Flieger abwehr kanone*) anti-tank gun appeared on the battlefield. Weighing 26.5 tons it had armour 13-78mm thick, a top speed of 15mph and a radius of action of 60 miles. It was 18ft 5ins long, 8ft 3ins high and 8ft 6ins wide. The four-man tank was basically armed with a 2 pounder and co-ax MG, but both the Matilda III CS & IV CS, mounted a 3-inch howitzer. The tank did not lend itself to mass production, but was nevertheless manufactured in considerable numbers during the early war years. Matilda was also the first British diesel-engined tank, being initially powered by twin 87hp AEC diesels (Mk I & Mk II), then later with twin six-cylinder 95hp Leyland water cooled petrol engines.

Once Matilda I was withdrawn, the A12 became known simply as Matilda and saw active service in Eritrea also with the Australians in New Guinea and the Western Desert, where it performed almost legendary tasks against the Italian armour - one Australian senior commander stating that each Matilda was worth a complete infantry battalion to him. The Matilda was almost immune to enemy fire except at point-blank range (a 7th RTR tank commander told the author that in one engagement he counted forty-six direct hits from Italian anti-tank guns without a single penetration). Sadly, its turret ring was too small to allow a larger gun to be fitted, so when the Afrika Korps arrived it was quickly outgunned by the PzKpfw IIIs and IVs.

Once it ceased to be used as a gun tank (mid-1942), Matildas continued in service as mine clear-

Above: **Matilda II, pushing Heavy Carrot mine clearing device – a 600lb demolition charge carried in front of AMRA and detonated remotely from the tank. Photographed at the Obstacle Assault Centre.** *(TM)*

Right: **Matilda II equipped with an early Scorpion Mk I mine flail, designed and produced between 1942 and 1943. The drum was driven by a auxiliary engine with the operator seated alongside. The Scorpion Mk II, had better side beams and was operated from inside the tank.** *(TM)*

ing vehicles (Baron), dozers, bridgelayers, even flamethrowers (Australian Matilda Frog). Probably the most interesting adaptation was the Matilda CDL (Canal Defence Light). This entailed fitting an extremely powerful searchlight housed in a special turret, on the Matilda chassis. The object of this strange and highly-secret device was to support night operations. By the end of 1942 five Royal Armoured Corps (RAC) regiments had been converted to the CDL role and undergone highly classified intensive training. The CDL was, however: 'the secret weapon that never quite made it' and it was never deployed in its intended role on D-Day. A few were used in 1945 to provide illumination for the Rhine Crossing.

Third of the early Infantry Tanks was a private venture designed by Leslie Little of Vickers Armstrongs. Contrary to the theory that the tank was accepted on St Valentine's Day and hence its name, it is strongly believed (by the firm at least) that its name was derived from the company's address: Vickers Armstrongs Ltd, Engineers Newcastle upon Tyne.

Despite being not particularly easy to handle – due to an uncomfortable driving position and effort required in operating the steering – the Valentine was reliable and well liked by its crews (three or four men depending upon Mark). Weighing 17 tons it was 17ft 9ins long, 7ft 5½ins

Above: **Valentine Mk I was the first model of the Infantry Tank Mk III and mounted a 2 pounder gun and co-ax BESA MG. Photographed on trials in Britain, 1939.** *(TM)*

high and 8ft 7½ins wide and was built in eleven different marks before being replaced. The tanks main attribute was that here at last was a chassis which had a turret ring large enough to allow it to be up-gunned. So, although the Mk I to VII were all armed with a 2 pounder plus MG, the Mk VIII, IX and X had a 6 pounder and the Mk XI a 75mm. The turret was large enough to accept the bigger gun but only at the expense of one crew member, this meant the commander had to load - a decided disadvantage. In looks the Valentine resembled an up-armoured A9 or A10 cruiser, but extra armour (up to 65mm) reduced its top speed to 15mph.

The Valentine chassis and running gear were also used to mount a wide variety of variants, including a scissors bridge , an SP gun (the 17 pounder Archer), a minefield clearance vehicle (Scorpion), a flame-thrower and a DD (Duplex-Drive) amphibious tank (used for training only). A total of 8,275 Valentines were built between 1940 and 1944 – 6,855 in Britain (accounting for almost twenty-five percent of wartime tank production) and 1,420 in Canada. All but thirty of the Canadian-built Valentines were supplied to the Soviet Union.

Valentine first saw action with the Eighth Army in the Western Desert and continued to be used there throughout all campaigns - some had covered over 3,000 miles on their tracks after El Alamein. A squadron (around fifteen tanks) was used in Madagascar, 1942 while others saw service with the New Zealanders in the Pacific.

Left: **A Valentine bridgelayer about to launch the 30ft scissors-type bridge. Later Valentines were replaced by the Churchill bridgelayer, although some were used in Burma.** (TM)

Right: **Valentine DD tanks with side-screens lowered. Those in the front are Mk IIIs while those to the rear are Mk VIII (up-gunned to 6 pounder).** *(TM)*

Below: **Valentine DD tanks loaded tightly in a Landing Craft Tank (LCT) on exercises. They were used only for training to perfect beach landing techniques, Sherman DDs being preferred for Normandy and other amphibious operations.** *(TM)*

In 1942-43, a decision was taken to produce a heavier version of the Valentine and design started on the A38 Valiant. The A38 weighed 27 tons and was 10 tons heavier with armour up to 112mm thick. The original design mounted a 6 pounder gun as its main armament but this was later replaced by a 75mm, complete with three-man crew turret. Only two were ever built - Valiant 1 powered by a 210hp GMC diesel engine and the Valiant 2 powered by a V-8 450 hp Rolls-Royce Meteorite petrol engine. The end of the war and success of the Centurion meant that the project was abandoned in 1945.

In September 1939, the first completely new British tank to be designed during the war began its existence in the shape of a General Staff outline specification for a new super heavy infantry tank, the A20. Its role would be to assist the infantry to dominate the World War One-type battlefield which, it was anticipated, would exist between the Maginot and Siegfried Lines. The original specification was as follows: Be resistant against enemy 37mm and 47 mm anti-tank ammunition, and 105 mm gun-howitzer ammunition at 100 yards range. Be able to cross a 16 foot wide trench and climb over a 7 foot high vertical obstacle. Have a maximum speed of 9mph and cross heavily shelled country at a speed of 5mph. Have a crew of eight - commander, driver, front gunner, four sponson

Left: **Last model of Valentine was the Mk XI which mounted a 75mm gun in place of the 6 pounder and was built in 1943. Note the new gun mantlet.** *(TM)*

Above: **The 27ton A38 Valiant was designed as an improved version of Valentine, but was 10 tons heavier. Underpowered it never entered production, being cancelled in 1945. The surviving A38 is in the Tank Museum, Bovington.** *(TM)*

Above: **Early Churchills on a training exercise in the New Forest, England - leading is a Mk I with a nose mounted 3-inch howitzer, others are Mk IIs with the howitzer removed and replaced by a BESA machine gun.** *(TM)*

Right: **Churchill Mk VI was a Mk IV modified as far as possible to Mk VIII standard, with a British version of the American 75mm gun, which could still fire US Army-type ammunition.** *(TM)*

gunners and a wireless operator. Armament was to be: one field gun in the front hull, two 2 pounders and 7.92mm BESA coaxially mounted in side sponsons, two 7.92mm BESA – one to fire to the rear and one to the front, to give all-round fire, and four 2 inch smoke mortars.

To all intents and purposes this was to be a modernised version of the heavy tank Mk VIII (the International) of 1918 vintage. The A20 prototype produced as a result of refining these specifications, bears some resemblance to both the International and to the eventual A22 Churchill.

Design ideas then diverged with the Super Heavy proposals giving rise, as we shall see, to TOG an 80-ton monster which proved unworkable. Then more realistically to the lighter 41-ton A22, designed to use Vauxhall Motors new 350hp Bedford Twin-Six engine.

Production was handed to Vauxhall, who now found themselves under pressure from the then Prime Minister (after whom the A22 would be named) to produce 500 to 600 tanks by Spring 1941. The revised specifications were swiftly approved and the tank given top production priority. By November 1940, a mock-up of the A22

infantry tank Mk IV was viewed by the Tank Design Board. By December, the first pilot model had appeared and was undergoing trials. In March 1941, the first production model in mild-steel was running. Early that summer, the new tank was officially named the Churchill and the first production models delivered to the Army on

Above: **Churchill AVRE, complete with dozer blade and 29 cm Petard mortar, which fired a 40-pound bomb (nicknamed Flying Dustbin) to a range of 80 yards.** *(TM)*

Left: **Churchill Mk IIs disembarking from an LCT during exercises on the Isle of Wight, southern England. Note that the 3-inch howitzer (originally in the nose) has been replaced by a BESA machine gun.** *(TM)*

Above: **Churchill ARK Mk II (British pattern) with ramps raised. The ramps and kingposts were longer than those on ARK Mk I.** *(TM)*

30 June 1941. These early Churchills were plagued with problems which took a year to rectify. Once this was achieved, it undoubtedly became the most important and adaptable British tank of World War Two.

In August 1942, Churchills first went into action during the ill-fated Dieppe raid. The landings were heavily opposed and tanks which did make it ashore found traction impossible on the steep shingle beach and were quickly immobilised, knocked out or captured, leaving the Germans as delighted owners of Britain's latest tank!

Six Mk IIIs were also shipped to the Middle East and were used in the second battle of El Alamein, Libya, October 1942. Here they proved to be immune to enemy anti-tank fire and capable of operating in desert conditions, before going on to operate successfully in Tunisia.

Eleven different Marks were produced and many variants, including the Gun Carrier 3 inch Mk I (3-inch AA gun became available when AA units re-equipped with the 3.7), the Crocodile flamethrower, various bridgelayers including three types of Ark, numerous experimental mine clearing and anti-mine devices, plus the Armoured Vehicle Royal Engineers (AVRE), Armoured Recovery Vehicles (ARV) and a Beach ARV (BARV).

Left: **Two Churchill Mk I ARKs in a deep gulley, one on top of the other, so as to bridge the gap. ARK could also be used to assist tanks to surmount other obstacles, like seawalls - a lesson learnt at Dieppe, France 19 July 1942.** *(TM)*

Left: **The Churchill flamethrower (Crocodile) was one of the best of its type in the world. Flame fuel was carried in a jettisonable trailer. It could fire 80, one second bursts up to a distance of between 80 and 120 yards. This photograph was taken near Belsen, Germany 1945.** *(TM)*

Right: **Black Prince A43, mounted a 17 pounder gun on a wider Churchill hull. Only six prototypes were built before the project was cancelled. Centurion Mk I proved to be a much superior tank.** *(TM)*

Below: **Churchill with a Farmer Deck plough device, mounted on a counter-weighted frame (seen here in the travelling position). This was one of a number of different types of plough used by the British 79th Armoured Division.** *(TM)*

Finally came the 'Super Churchill', offically called Black Prince A43, which was in essence a heavier (49tons), wider (by 2ft), slower (11mph), wider tracked (by 10ins) Churchill Mk VII, fitted with a 17-pounder OQF gun.

Heavy Tanks

The British produced only two tanks during World War Two which could be classified as Heavy Tanks. The first of these, known simply as TOG, has already been mentioned in the early saga of the Churchill. At 33ft 3ins long, 10ft high and 10ft 3ins wide, the 80-ton TOG was (and still is) the heaviest British tank ever built and owes its design to an intrepid band of old World War One warriors - Stern, Wilson, Swinton, d'Eyncourt, Ricardo, Symes and Tritton, who were known collectively as 'The Old Gang' - hence the name TOG. Their

Above: **Churchill AVRE carrying a large fascine used for filling ditches and bomb craters. The AVRE had a steel fascine cradle bolted to its nose, with a release slip line, operated from the turret.** *(TM)*

Churchill Tanks		
Mark	Weight (tons)	Main armament and Remarks
I	38.5	2 pounder in turret, 3inch howitzer in nose
II	same	2 pounder in turret, 3inch howitzer replaced by MG
IICS	same	as for Mk I, but with gun positions reversed
All the above had fully-exposed tracks and engine intake louvres		
III	39	6 pounder in new welded turret
IV	same	6 pounder in new cast turret
IV (NA 75)		as above with the American 75mm gun
V	same	95mm howitzer in place of 6pounder
VI	same	British 75mm in place of 6pounder
VII	40	thicker armour, new cast/welded heavy turret, heavier suspension, better gearbox, 75mm gun and other modifications
VIII	same	as for the Mk VII but with a 95mm howitzer
IX		up-armoured Mk II & IV
X	same	up-armoured Mk VI
XI	same	up-armoured and up-dated Mk V

Above: **Ardeer Aggie, an experimental vehicle based on Churchill Mk III fitting a more powerful Petard mortar.** *(TM)*

Below: **Churchill AVRE fitted with CIRD (Canadian Indestructible Roller Device).** *(TM)*

tank was designed to fight a battle which never materialised, the Blitzkrieg tactics of the Panzerwaffe obviating the World War One-type of static trench warfare which they had envisaged. Despite its great weight, massive V-12 600hp Paxman Ricard diesel engine, highly complex steering and transmission, the monster initially mounted a 2 pounder gun in a Matilda II turret! This was replaced on TOG II by a Challenger turret mounting a 17 pounder gun. Only two models were built by Fosters of Lincoln between 1939 and 1941, the project being shelved in 1944.

The four main tank building nations of World War Two: Germany, Great Britain, the United States and the Soviet Union, all built super heavy tanks/tank destroyers towards the end of the war. Germany was the only one to succeed in getting such a weapon into operational service with its 70ton JagdTiger. The British equivalent, the 75 ton A39 Tortoise, which mounted a 32 pounder gun, carried a crew of seven and achieved a top speed of 12mph, had only reached the pilot stage by 1944 despite the fact that it had been first projected in 1942. Six pilot models were eventually produced in 1946, so the tank played no part in wartime operations.

A last word – In July 1944, Field Marshal Montgomery then commander of 21st Army

Group, formally proposed that the division between cruiser and infantry tanks should be abolished. This did not happen until 1946, so although the Centurion medium gun tank made its appearance before VE-Day, there was no official end to the problem which had bedevilled British tank development since well before the outbreak of war. The inescapable comment which has to be made on British tank design and production during World War Two is: too many models, most of which were under-gunned, under-armoured and, with only a few exceptions, well below the standard of their German armoured counterparts.

Top: **Tortoise, the A39 heavy assault tank, only six were built in pilot form.** *(TM)*

Above: **TOG 2 as it is today at the Tank Museum, Bovington.** *(TM)*

Left: **TOG 1 had a Matilda II turret mounting only a 2 pounder gun. This was replaced on TOG 2 with a Challenger turret mounting a 17 pounder gun.** *(TM)*

CHAPTER TWO

British Commonwealth

It soon became apparent after the débâcle of France, that Britain would be hard pressed to build sufficient tanks for its own defence, so the nations of the Commonwealth would have to fend for themselves.

I f Great Britain was in a desperate state for tanks at the outbreak of World War Two, then its Commonwealth and Empire partners were even worse off. Australia, could possibly claim to have had a hand in the invention of the first tank. In 1912, the engineer Lancelot de Mole submitted a design to the War Office for an armoured fighting vehicle, but his ideas had been filed away and apparently forgotten.

Later in 1927, Australia formed its own Tank Corps, but the force was not improved or enlarged until 1939. At the outbreak of war, their Armoured Corps were equipped with just four obsolete Vickers Medium tanks and some twenty plus obsolescent British-built light tanks, together with a few armoured car units.

In New Zealand, the army had nothing - armoured warfare was not even taught to anyone in its small armed forces.

On the other side of the world Canada was just as badly off, with sixteen British-built Light Mk VIs and twelve or so Carden-Loyd carriers dating from 1931. Although six Canadian regiments had been designated for the armoured role, Brigadier 'Worthy' Worthington, MC & Bar, MM & Bar, (who was destined to become the 'father' of the Canadian Armoured Corps) had yet to get involved in its formation and this did not happen until August 1940.

India had witnessed the disbandment of all the British RTC light tank companies and the beginning of the mechanisation of the Indian cavalry in 1937. This was still not yet entirely complete, although, thanks to the invaluable help of the RTC training cadres, the process was well under way. However, as no new equipment had been supplied, their obsolescent AFVs were all outdated by modern battlefield standards.

CANADA

At the outbreak of the war, Canada found itself short of the tanks needed to equip their armoured formations, but could not immediately rely on either Britain or the United States to supply them. Tanks were in such short supply that the Canadians purchased for training all the obsolete tanks (219 in total) they could from the US Army. These were mainly the M1917 Ford 6 ton (US copy of the French Renault FT17 light tank), but there were also some Heavy Mk VIII (International). It is reputed that Canada paid 'scrap iron' prices ($20 a ton) for them.

Nevertheless, they did have heavy industrial potential, so when it was decided by the British to increase tank production, a major order was placed by them with the Canadian Pacific Railway Company of Montreal (CPR), to build Valentines. The Defence Department also placed an order with CPR for 488 Valentines to equip the 1st Canadian Armoured Brigade. However, by the time they were completed the Brigade was in Britain and all the Canadian Valentine produc-

tion tanks, less some thirty retained for training purposes, were delivered to the Soviet Union. In total, just over 1,400 Valentines were built by CPR.

Canada also decided to design and build a cruiser tank (as did Australia), to be based largely upon the American M3 medium tank, but with British and Canadian improvements - for example, without the high silhouette or the sponson-mounted main armament. Initially it was decided to arm the tank with the British 2 pounder gun, although it was designed from the outset to accept the 6 pounder. The new cruiser tank would be called Ram, in honour of General 'Worthy' Worthington (the Ram was part of his family crest) founder of the Canadian armoured forces, and would be built at a new Tank Arsenal in Montreal.

A prototype was completed in June 1941 and the following month, one of the newly-completed prototypes was sent to the Aberdeen Proving Ground (APG) in Maryland for evaluation. How much influence the Ram had on the eventual design of Sherman has never been satisfactorily resolved. Ram Mk I (19ft long, 8ft 9ins high and 9ft 1in wide) went into production, the first fifty mounting the 2 pounder, the 6 pounder was then fitted and the tank became Ram Mk II. Over 1000 Rams were produced but were never used in action as a gun tank, most being used for training in Canada and Britain. The United States, as for Australia, was able to supply sufficient tanks from its vast production capability.

Nevertheless, the Ram Mk II did see action as open-topped armoured personnel carriers (APC), known for obvious reasons as Kangaroos. These tanks had their turrets removed and rungs welded to the sides of the vehicle to allow for easy access. The interior could accommodate a section of eleven soldiers and were used to great effect by the British 79th Armoured Division. Some Ram Kangaroos were fitted with flamethrowers in place of the hull MG and named Badgers. Also there were Ram Command/ OP tanks, ARVs, AVREs and various special fittings including a 3.7inch AA gun, a 75mm gun and even a 40 inch searchlight! However, probably best known was the Sexton, 25 pounder SP gun, which was usually accompanied by a Wallaby Ram (a stripped out Sexton) ammunition carrier.

When Ram production ended at the CPR works in mid-1943, work began on the Canadian version of the American M4 Sherman medium tank, this was to be known as the Grizzly. The tank was based on the M4A1 with a cast hull, and was basically an 'assembly job' as most of its components were shipped directly from the United States. Total production was just under 200 tanks and these saw service with Canadian armoured units in their own country, also in Europe. There was one other variant of the Grizzly, an AA version known as Skink, this mounted four 20 mm Polsten cannons and associated sighting equipment. The Skink came into being due to the requirement for AA protection, which existed up to 1943 but diminished as Allied air superiority grew in 1944. Only a few Skinks were built before production was cancelled.

Above: **A heavily ladened Ram Kangaroo APC passing a well-protected Churchill. The Kangaroo was a stripped out Ram and could carry a full infantry section of eleven men and their equipment.** *(TM)*

Far right: **Grizzly I was basically an American M4A1 medium tank assembled in Canada from American parts.** *(TM)*

Right: **Ram Mk II, mounted a 6 pounder gun plus a co-ax .30in Browning machine gun and another in the hull.** *(TM)*

Right: **The first fifty Rams to be built were Mk Is mounting, as shown here, a 2 pounder gun.** *(TM)*

Below: **Ram OP/Command, was designed as an armoured observation post or command vehicle. It was fitted with a dummy gun, extra radio equipment and telephone reels. Only 84 were built.** *(TM)*

AUSTRALIA

The Australian Cruiser (AC 1) tank, known as Sentinel, came into being because the Australian Ministry of Munitions decided early in the war that they would be unable to rely upon Britain or the United States to provide them with the military equipment needed should Japan attack. After the débâcle in France, Britain was hard pressed to find sufficient tanks for its own defence, as was the then still uncommitted United States whose great industrial potential was not as yet, geared to war production. Therefore, despite the fact that Australia did not even manufacture its own motor cars, had only limited engineering facilities and no background experience, they bravely decided to design and build their own tanks.

In 1940, they dispatched one of their ordnance production engineers, Mr A Chamberlain, to the United States to study tank production. About the same time a British tank design expert, Colonel W D Watson, joined the Australian Army Design Directorate. A third tank expert, Frenchman R Perrier, had also arrived in Australia having escaped from Japan. The three, Chamberlain, Watson and Perrier, would be responsible for designing and producing the Sentinel tank - a remarkable achievement.

The General Staff (GS) issued a specification in November 1940 calling for a four or five-man tank, weighing between 16 and 20 tons, with armour 50mm thick, a top speed of 30mph and armed with a 2 pounder gun and two machine guns. It was anticipated that 2,000 would be needed, with first deliveries in July 1941 and a production target of around ten tanks a day.

Both Watson and Chamberlain, who had met briefly in the United States, were impressed with the mechanical components of the M3 medium tank, agreeing that it should form the basis of the Australian Cruiser and subsequently proposed incorporating many of its parts.

Above: **Skink, an adaptation of the Canadian Grizzly tank, was designed to defend armour from air attack during the assault on occupied Europe.** *(TM)*

Left: **An Australian Matilda Dozer, fitted with a box-shaped blade, at work in New Guinea.** *(TM)*

Above: **Sentinel AC III was a test vehicle with two 25 pounder guns in a co-axial mount. Fired together they produced only 20 percent more recoil than a 17pounder.** *(TM)*

Unfortunately, great difficulty was experienced in manufacturing the components and casting the armour, so the AC 1 design was shelved in favour of a new, lighter model in the 16 to 18 ton range designated AC 2, which Chamberlain was mainly responsible for designing. This was also found to be impractical because of difficulties in obtaining American components so, in September 1940, the AC 1 design was resurrected. The engine layout, devised by Perrier, involved using three V-8 Cadillac truck engines in a 'clover-leaf' pattern coupled to a transfer box beneath the turret and then via a single drive-shaft to a front-mounted gearbox. This novel engine arrangement produced 330hp, sufficient to give the tank a top speed of 40mph (governed to 30mph on production models). The choice of Hotchkiss suspension was most probably made by Perrier.

A wooden mock-up was built in early 1941 and by October that year, the first hull had been cast and all transmission teething troubles corrected. The first three pilot models were completed in January 1942 and the first production vehicle in August 1942 – just twenty-two months after the issue of the original GS specifications! The Chullona Tank Assembly Shops in New South Wales would build only sixty-six Sentinels (20ft 9ins long, 8ft 5ins high and 9ft 1in wide) before production ended in July 1943. There were some inherent problems with the tank – such as the bogie-wheel tyres, turret drive gear, engine cooling system and poor firepower, although this was rectified in later models when both the 25 pounder (twin guns, AC III) and 17 pounder gun (AC IV) were fitted. However, the main reason for its demise was the fact that it was soon established that America was able to supply as many tanks as were needed to fully equip the 1st Australian Armoured

Left: **Matilda Mk IVs of 1st Australian Tank Battalion (later the 1st Armoured Regiment) on manoeuvres, preparing for action against the Japanese in Finschafen, New Guinea, 1943. The leading tank is the close support version mounting a 3-inch howitzer.** *(TM)*

Right: **A standard production AC I Sentinel. An outstanding engineering achievement, had it been up-gunned to a 17 pounder, as was proposed, it would have been a formidable tank.** *(TM)*

Division, while the British also now had spare tank production capacity.

The AC 1 Sentinel was from then on only used for training, whilst Australian armoured units employed both British and American tanks, including Matildas, Valentines, Grants and M3 lights.

Later they received enough Churchills to equip a regiment, but these arrived too late to be used in action. The Australians also locally modified various tanks including: Matilda Frog and Matilda Murray - both flamethrower conversions for use in New Guinea. Matilda dozer, also for

New Guinea and Grant ARV Mk II - conversion of standard American Grant into an ARV, by removing its armament and installing a winch, earth spade, and other equipment.

NEW ZEALAND

Amazingly, New Zealand also decided in 1940 to manufacture its own tanks when it was found that they could not be supplied by Britain. The first attempt led to the fitting of a box-like corrugated

Below: **Matilda Frog flamethrower of the 2nd Battalion 1st Australian Armoured Brigade Reconnaissance Squadron, moving towards the oil refineries at Balikpapan, July 1945.** *(TM)*

armour structure over an International Harvester caterpillar-tracked farm tractor, which gave the resulting 20 to 25 ton mobile pillbox 'tank' a height of twelve feet. The intention was for it – now called the Bob Semple Tank (named after the government minister responsible), to be armed with machine guns (Brens) which could be fired through six loopholes (two in front, one each side, one at the rear and finally one in a small turret). For all this firepower the tank had to carry a large crew of eight men . Only four were built and were quickly found to be a total failure, being top heavy and highly unstable whilst moving. Soon they became the subject of public ridicule due to their 'Heath Robinson' appearance - for example, the gunner in the front had to lie face-down on a mattress, on top of the engine to fire his weapon!

For the war, New Zealand armoured units were then mainly equipped with US-built tanks, as were the armoured regiments in the rest of the Commonwealth, including India and South Africa.

Above: **Matilda II of 2nd Battalion, 4th Australian Armoured Regiment on the Buin Road, Bougainville, New Guinea, April 1945. Note the spotlight mounted next to the driver's hatch.** *(TM)*

Left: **Bob Semple Tank. Built in New Zealand between 1940 and 1941. Only four of these strange looking mobile pillboxes were ever produced.** *(TM)*

CHAPTER THREE

Germany

'The tank forces are at once the youngest of all the arms, and the one with the highest degree of such striking power. They must therefore advance their claims on their own account, since there is no country in the world where the other arms will concede these of their own free will.'

Heinz Guderian (extract from 'Achtung Panzer!', published 1937)

During World War One Germany showed minimal interest in tanks and tank warfare, building only a handful of the cumbersome 30-ton A7V, and making relatively ineffectual use of captured British and French tanks. However, certain influential German officers did appreciate the tank's true potential and were determined to see that next time this would be used to the full. And, despite the shackles of the Versailles Treaty, they were determined that there would be 'a next time', and that the Fatherland would achieve even greater glory, with the tank playing a major role.

By using subterfuge and double dealing, materially helped by the willingness of war-weary Europe to refrain from investigating the true purpose of, for example, such quasi-agricultural items as the 'tractoren' they were building, Germany secretly began to rearm. Of course, once the Nazis came to power, most of this subterfuge was swept aside and they started to openly design and build tanks. The nation's vast heavy manufacturing industry, centred on the Krupp empire in the Ruhr, was only too delighted to assist, while their soldiers avidly seized upon the teachings of the British tank pioneers, such as Liddell Hart and Fuller, to formulate the ways in which the new weapons could be used to best advantage. The tactics of Blitzkrieg would be developed from such teachings by men like Heinz Guderian, who was one of the major architects in the development of the Panzer force. Initially, however, he did not have

it all his own way, there being just as much suspicion and prejudice against mechanisation in the German Army as there was in Britain and the United States.

However, Guderian had a major advantage and that was the full support of his Führer. Hitler having watched one of Guderian's early tank demonstrations, is reputed to have exclaimed excitedly: 'That's what I need! That's what I'm going to have!' Although, as we shall see, he meddled in both the design and production of tanks, as well as in the running of the Panzer armies, Hitler never lost his enthusiasm for the tank nor his conviction that they would always win battles.

With typical German thoroughness, the tank building industry and the military hierarchy, laid down a system for classifying vehicles, which included the following rules for tanks. Experimental machines were always given a serial number, the first two figures indicating the vehicle's weight, while the last two were the prototype number. The prefix 'VK' (*Volkettenfahrzeuge* - fully-tracked vehicle) was added and sometimes, a letter or letters in brackets afterwards, to indicate the builder. For example, VK4001(H) would indicate the first prototype of a 40-ton tank built by Henschel. Once in service a tank was designated as a *PanzerKampfwagen* (armoured fighting vehicle), which was abbreviated to 'PzKpfw' or 'PzKw', plus a Roman numeral (I-VI) to indicate to which class (light, medium, heavy) the tank belonged. Within each class a letter was added to denote which model (*Ausführung*) it was, starting with A – PzKpfw III

Above: **An abandoned Panther on a street in a Russian town. This is an Ausf G, the last production model, which had the driver's vision port removed from the front glacis in order to increase strength.** *(TM)*

Ausf C – third model of *PanzerKampfwagen* III model C. In addition, every vehicle accepted into service was given an Ordnance Inventory Number – *Sonderkraftfahrzeug* abbreviated to SdKfz. A small number of tanks were also given nicknames, the most well known being 'Tiger' for PzKpfw VI and 'Panther' for PzKpfw V.

From the early 1930s, German industry had begun tank production in earnest: Krupp, for example, were ordered by Hitler to build 100 new light tanks by March 1934, to be followed by another 650 the following year. The pace of tank building quickened and by 1935 the first three Panzer divisions had been formed and had received their new tanks, although most of them were, like their British equivalents, too small, too lightly armed and too thinly armoured for combat, and only really suitable for training. However, two larger models were already under construction – the *Zugführerswagen* (ZW) company commander's vehicle and the *Bataillonführerswagen* (BW) battalion commander's vehicle - these codenames being used so as to hide their true purpose. From 1939, they became known as the PzKpfw III and IV respectively, quickly becoming the backbone of the growing Panzer divisions. Their basic construction was such that, without major alteration, they could easily accept larger guns and thicker armour, enabling them to remain both in production and service throughout the war. During the period 1934 to 1938, the Germans built a total of 4,110 tanks of all types (including

those they seized from Czechoslovakia), however, by skillful propaganda this figure was greatly inflated, so that the rest of the world was convinced that Germany had a far larger tank force than actually existed. When the Germans began their invasion of France in May 1940 the Deuxieme Bureau estimated that they has between 7000 and 7500 tanks. This figure came to be extensively used to justify the swift collapse of France.

When Germany attacked Poland, the total number of tanks they had in service, but not including those they had taken from the Czechs, was just 3,195, of which PzKpfw I and IIs amounted to all but some 300, there being only 98 PzKpfw IIIs and 211 PzKpfw IVs in operational units. Most of the Panzer force was involved in the thirty day campaign during which 217 were destroyed (eighty-nine Mk I, eighty-three Mk II, twenty-six Mk III and nineteen Mk IV). Tank production continued to rise, the monthly average for 1939 was 140 vehicles, this figure had increased to 720 per month by 1944. Even this figure was not sufficient to meet the demands of the Wehrmacht. Precious production capacity was also wasted by building such preposterous super-heavy tank projects as E-100 and Maus. In addition Germany could never hope to match the output of the United States or the Soviet Union, both of whom consistently outproduced them, despite the fact that the former had to start its tank building industry virtually from scratch, while the latter had to continually move many of its major tank factories

GERMAN TANK PRODUCTION 1939-1945

Year	Total
1939	1,680
1940	1,459
1941	3,256
1942	4,098
1943	6,083
1944	8,466
1945	988
Total	26,030

Note: This total figure can be almost doubled, to over 47,000 if one includes all other tank chassis based AFVs, such as assault guns, assault artillery, tank destroyers, self-propelled guns, etc.

Above: **Between the wars the Germans used civilian cars (Dixi/Adler/NSU) fitted with canvas and wood 'tank' bodies for training purposes.** *(TM)*

as the enemy advanced. Nevertheless, it is a tribute to German design and production skills that their tanks were, on the whole, superior to anything built by the Allies, although they did tend to be over complicated and subject to minor faults – especially, for example, in the bitter cold winters on the Eastern Front. However, in general terms, German tanks were masters of the battlefield. In addition, and equally importantly, their crews were extremely well trained, thoroughly professional in their approach to warfare and, at least for most of the war, with a high morale and well motivated. This had a great deal to do with the high esteem in which they were held by the German people. Developing the 'Panzer spirit' was vital and, as one Panzer commander told the author, the killing of an enemy tank was regarded as the achievement of the entire crew. Confident,

LIGHT TANKS

In 1933, the Heereswaffenamt (Army Weapons Branch), issued a requirement for the development of a 5 ton, lightly armoured tank (proof against small arms fire) and to be armed with two machine guns in a small, fully traversing turret. Five companies were invited to tender and eventually the Krupp design was chosen. Two firms were selected to oversee the project – Krupp AG of Essen, for the chassis and running gear, and Daimler-Benz AG of Berlin-Marienfelde, for the superstructure and turret. The LKA 1 (code name *Landswirtschaftlicher Schlepper* (LaS) meant Agriculture Tractor), was based largely on the British Carden-Loyd tan-

Left : **A PzKpfw I Ausf A. Over 2 tons lighter than the Ausf B, its suspension comprised a sprocket, four road wheels and a slightly larger fifth road wheel which acted as the idler, plus three top rollers. The photograph is of a brand new diesel engined Ausf A taken at the Henshel works, Kassel, Germany.** *(TM)*

kette, and the first three prototypes built in late 1933 were tested in early 1934. The earliest versions had no turrets (*ohne Aufbau* – without superstructure) but were ideally suited for driver training. Quantity production began at the Henschel works, Kassel in July 1934, the first contract being for 150 vehicles. In total, 477 PzKpfw I Ausf A (SdKfz 101) were built between 1933 and 1934, making it Germany's first mass produced tank. Their vulnerability was fully appreciated from the start; nevertheless, like their British equivalents, they would soon be used in action on the battlefield.

The Ausf A soon proved to be underpowered and was replaced by a more powerful model, which was slightly longer, thus requiring a modified chassis and running gear. The Ausf B was first issued to units in 1935 and went on in

quantity production until 1939, although some component manufacture continued for two further years. Around 1,500 were built, including a number of *ohne Aufbau*, for driver training.

PzKpfw I		
Mark	Ausf A	Ausf B
Date of origin	1934	1935
Weight (ton)	5.4	6
Dimensions		
Length:	13ft 2^1/2ins	14ft 6ins
Height:	5ft 7ins	5ft 7ins
Width:	6ft 9ins	6ft 9ins
Crew	two	two
Armament	two 7.92mm MG 13 in fully traversing turret	
Armour	6-13 mm	6-13 mm
Engine	57hp Krupp M304	100hp Maybach NL38TR
Max speed	22mph	25mph
Range	90 miles	87.5 miles

There were a number of variants which used either the Ausf A or Ausf B chassis, these included an ammunition carrier, an armoured bridgelayer, an armoured flamethrower, a self-propelled infantry gun, a self-propelled anti-tank gun and a demolition charge laying tank.

Both Ausf A & Ausf B saw operational service with the Condor Legion in support of General Franco's Nationalists in Spain, there being around 120 within a tank force, commanded by Colonel Ritter von Thoma. Although this did give the Panzertruppe some battle experience, it also showed that the little tanks were highly vulnerable and led to some false assumptions being made about the correct organisation and use of tanks - but not

Far left **A Kleiner Panzer Befelswagen, photographed after the Blitzkrieg on Poland. This was the first armoured command tank and had a fixed turret, occupied by an extra crewman (radio operator) and the radio equipment. Between 1935 and 1937 a total of 190 were produced.** *(TM)*

Left: **Despite thin armour and minimal armament which made them vulnerable in battle, the PzKpfw I Ausf A & Ausf B proved to be excellent training tanks. Both types saw action in Poland and France, but were phased out as gun tanks by 1941.** *(TM)*

Above: **Some driver training vehicles were modified to run on gas – note the gas cylinders on the sides of this PzKpfw I Ausf B ohne Aufbau.** *(TM)*

Two other models were produced, the Ausf C and Ausf F. The former (originally known as VK601) was designed as a fast reconnaissance vehicle with thicker armour (10-30mm) and better armament (2cm gun replacing one of the MGs). It weighed 8 ton, had a top speed of nearly 50 mph and a range of 188 miles. Forty were built by Krauss-Maffei, the order being completed by 1942, but only a handful ever saw any combat, most being issued to reserve units. The Ausf F (VK 1801) was derived from the VK601 development in 1939, but had much thicker armour so that it could be used for the close infantry support. With a combat weight over 20 tons but powered by the same engine as Ausf C the 150hp Maybach H l45P, its top speed was drastically reduced to 15 mph and its range to under 100 miles. Some were combat evaluated in Russia, but do not appear to have ever been used in action.

The *Kleiner panzer befelswagen* (Kl Pz Bef Wg) SdKfz 265, the command version, was developed mainly from Ausf B, although a few Ausf A were also modified. This comprised removing the standard turret and installing in its place a fixed, built-up superstructure which provided room for another radio set (the ultra short wave FuG 6), a radio operator and a small map table. It was armed with one ball-mounted MG34. Between 1935-37, 200 were built and issued to Panzer unit headquarters and remained in service until late 1942.

When it became clear that the two new medium tanks - the *Zugführerswagen* and the *Bataillonführerswagen* would not be ready as early as anticipated, it was decided to build another light training tank, which would be relatively cheap and easy to produce, but with a larger gun and better armour than the PzKpfw I. The development contracts were issued in 1934 for a tank in the 10 ton class, to three manufacturers – Krupp, Henschel and MAN and, after assessing their proposals, MAN was chosen to develop the chassis and Daimler Benz the superstructure and turret, while other manufacturers were brought in

by the Germans. It was the French and the Russians who interpreted limited tank involvement incorrectly. The PzKpfw Is were next deployed during Anschluss – the 'peaceful annexation' of Austria in 1938, where they motored over 400 miles and did not fire a shot. There were many breakdowns, which surprisingly proved a blessing in disguise, as it led to a complete reorganisation of the repair and recovery services needed to support the Panzer divisions. Any misgivings which resulted from these operations were quickly dispelled when the Blitzkrieg tactics the Polish and French campaigns showed the true value of the new arm. The little tanks were also used in the invasion of Norway and Denmark, then in Russia and North Africa, but were soon relegated to training or modified to other purposes.

Right: **A PzKpfw II Ausf b heading infantry into action. This model and the earlier Ausf a/1, a/2 & a/3 all saw action in Poland as main battle tanks, but were later relegated to the reconnaissance role.** *(TM)*

Left: *Ladungsleger auf* **PzKpfw I Ausf B**, demolition laying version of the PzKpfw I. The demolition charge was released down a chute at the rear of the tank. *(TM)*

Above and left: **PzK pfw II Ausf A, B and C**, all had five independently sprung, larger diameter road wheels instead of the earlier six small road wheels. Armament was a 20mm cannon with a co-ax MG 34. *(TM)*

to assist. The tanks in the first production run of twenty-five vehicles were known as the PzKpfw II Ausf A1 (SdKfz 121), also known as the 1/LaS 100, weighed only 7.2 tons, well within the 10 ton limit. It had a crew of three and was armed with a 2cm KwK 30 automatic gun and a co-axially mounted 7.92mm MG 34 machine gun, which from then on became the standard tank machine gun in place of the MG 13. The 130 hp Maybach HL57TR engine gave it a top speed of 25mph and a range of 125 miles. Two further batches of Ausf a were built - twenty-five a/2 and then fifty a/3, both of which had minor improvements to the engine cooling, tracks and suspension.

There followed two more small batches of development models, each improving on the last one, the first being the Ausf B (100 built between February and March 1937) and then the Ausf C (built from March 1937) the final development model before the tank entered mass production. The most visible feature this development was a change to the suspension from small roadwheels and girder assembly, to one with five medium-sized, independently sprung wheels below four return rollers. The Ausf A was the first production model (from July 1937), followed by Ausf B (December 1937) and Ausf C (from June 1938), over 1,100 completed by April 1940. This was the

most numerous type of tank in service at the outbreak of the war and bore the brunt of the fighting in both Poland and France, suffering in the same fate as PzKpfw I, being under-armoured and under-gunned.

PzKpfw II			
Mark	Ausf A, B & C	Ausf D & E (a)	Ausf F (b)
Date of origin	1937	1938	1941
Weight (tons)	8.9	10	9.5
Dimensions			
Length	15ft 9¹/₂ins	15ft 2¹/₂ins	15ft 9¹/₂ins
Height	6ft 6ins	6ft 7ins	7ft 2ins
Width	7ft 3ins	7ft 3¹/₂ins	7ft 3ins
Crew	three	three	three
Main Armament			
	one 2cm KwK 30	both – one 2cm KwK L/55	
Secondary (all tanks)	one MG 34		
Armour (mm)	5–15(c)	5–30	15–35
Engine HL62TR	135hp HL62TRM (all Maybachs)	140hp HL62TR	135hp
Max speed	25mph	35mph	25mph
Range	125 miles	125 miles	125miles

Notes: (a) designed originally for the mechanised cavalry, some were converted to flamethrowers. (b) final production model. (c) from 1940, extra 20mm plates bolted onto front glacis.

The Ausf D/E was also known as the *Schnellkampfwagen* (fast fighting vehicle), it had torsion bar suspension with four large double-tyred road wheels and fitted a more powerful engine. It was due to be issued to *Leichte* (light) divisions, but in the end less than fifty were produced. The final production model, the Ausf F, was built exclusively by FAMO of Breslau, the most important change being the up-armouring of the front to 35mm and sides to 20mm. A dummy visor was also added, presumably to draw fire away from the driver's visor.

Above: **Red Army tankmen use captured German AFVs. Leading this column of StuG's, photographed on 7 July 1942, is a PzKpfw III Ausf J.** *(TM)*

Left: **American GIs have taken over this PzKpfw II and painted a white Allied star on its turret.** *(TM)*

Far left: **A PzKpfw III Ausf E in France, May 1940. Ausf E was the first in extended production just under 100 being built between December 1938 and October 1939. Main armament was a 37mm gun.** *(TM)*

Left: **PzKpfw III Ausf K *Befelswagen*. This version came into service in 1942 and was an adaptation of the normal gun tank.** *(TM)*

Right: **Red Army soldiers drag German tanks off the battlefield near Stalingrad, January 1943. The nearest is a PzKpfw III Ausf E, the first model with six road wheels and torsion bar suspension, which became standard on all Panzer IIIs.** *(TM)*

Right: **Kicking up the snow of a bitter Russian winter, this PzKpfw III Ausf H was built between October 1940 and April 1941. It was the first model to mount the 50mm KwK L./42 gun.** *(TM)*

Below: **First of the highly successful PzKpfw III series was Ausf A, which had five large road wheels. Only 10 were built in 1937. Also known as the 1** *Serie Zugführerwagen.* *(GF)*

There was some further development after the Ausf F which included the following:

Ausf G, light reconnaissance tank initially known as neuer Art VK 901 which weighed some 9.2 ton, had yet another redesigned suspension with five pairs of overlapping roadwheels and torsion bar suspension. Twelve were built and the only operational service they saw was when some of their turrets were used as static pillboxes.

Ausf J, the VK 1601 was an attempt to up-date the little tank as much as possible (without altering its basic features) by increasing its armoured protection - front to 80mm, sides and

Left: **A British Officer in the Western Desert examining the vehicle pennant from this knocked-out PzKpfw III. The Totenkopf (Death's Head skull and crossbones) was the collar badge of the Panzertruppe. Over 15,000 Panzer III chassis were built between 1935 and 1945.** *(TM)*

Left: **Soviet troops inspecting an abandoned PzKpfw III Ausf J, in June 1942. The Ausf J still mounted the 50mm gun, but had thicker armour front and rear than previous models.** *(TM)*

rear to 50mm and top to 25mm, putting up the combat weight to 18tonnes. Fitted with a 150hp Maybach HL45P engine, it had a top speed of 20mph. Over twenty were produced in 1942, but few saw operational service.

Ausf H & M, light reconnaisance tanks (VK 903 & VK 1301), but heavier – 10.5 tons, with a different engine (Maybach HL66P) and a new gearbox. Neither model saw operational service.

Ausf L, the Luchs (Lynx) SdKfz 123 was produced from experience gained from the Ausf G & J. It looked like the VK 901, but had a combat weight of just under 13 tons. Although 800 were

Left: **Additional spaced armour fitted to the turret and sides of a PzKpfw III. This was designed as extra protection against attack by HEAT weapons such as the American Bazooka and the British PIAT.** *(TM)*

Below: **This PzKpfw III Ausf L mounts a long-barrelled 5cm KwK 39 L/60 gun, the second model to do so. A total of 650 were built in the last half of 1942.** *(TM)*

Below centre: **Taken from the pages of *Signal*, Hitler's wartime picture magazine, the photograph shows the vital components of the German Blitzkrieg in action in Russia, 1942, armoured infantry (*Panzergrenadier*) and tanks, advancing with artillery and dive bomber support.** *(TM)*

Left: **The *Kleiner Panzerbefels- wagen* was developed specifically as an armoured command vehicle, based on the PzKpfw I Ausf B. This Kl Pz Bef Wg served with the *Deutsches Afrika Korps* between 1941-42, was captured in the desert, taken to Britain and inspected in detail at Farnborough in 1943.** *(TM)*

Below: **Another view of the Tank Museum's PzKpfw III Ausf L, this time painted in the colours of the *Afrika Korps*. It is still in running order. The Ausf L first saw action in Russia in 1942.** *(TM)*

Right: **The first PzKpfw VI, Tiger Ausf E, to be captured complete by the British in Tunisia, is seen here on Horse Guards Parade London, in November 1944. Hitler once said; 'A battalion on Tigers is worth a normal Panzer Division.'** *(TM)*

Right: **The Tank Museum's PzKpfw IV shows all the hallmarks of good tank design, in that it has been up-gunned with the long-barrelled 75mm KwK40 L/48, up-armoured on the hull front and fitted with spaced armour around the turret. PzKpfw IVs were in production from 1937 to 1945.** *(TM)*

Below: **The awe-inspiring front view of a Tiger I, its 88mm gun capable of defeating 90mm of armour plate at 2,300 metres. Tiger carried 92 rounds of mixed ammunition (AP & HE) for its main gun.** *(TM)*

Above: **Panther's clean lines are very obvious on this excellent photograph of an Ausf A, of which 2,000 were built between 1943-44. Panther was designed to counter the threat posed by the Soviet T-34.** *(TM)*

Left: **Tiger II, also known as the** *Königstiger* **(King Tiger or Royal Tiger) was an even more formidable tank. This version seen in the Tank Museum at Bovington, is fitted with the Porsche turret. Only the first 50 built had this turret, the remaining 439 had the Henschel type.** *(TM)*

Above: This Panther, PzKpfw V Ausf A has been captured undamaged by the Red Army and is being driven at speed (possibly on test) - its top speed was just under 29mph. *(TM)*

initially ordered only 100 were built (between September 1943 and January 1944) before the project was cancelled. It had a crew of four and a top speed of 37.5mph; it saw operational service with reconnaissance units.

In addition, the PzKpfw II was converted to various other uses such as self-propelled artillery (mounting numerous guns – the 15cm SiG 33 L/12; 7.62cm PaK 36 L/51.5; 7.5cm PaK 40/2 and 10.5cm le FH18M L/28 Wespe), bridgelayer, SP anti-tank gun and, most successfully, as a flame-thrower. The PzKpfw II Flamm Ausf A and B (Sd Kfz 122) were both converted from gun tanks and also built from scratch. The 150 in service were used to deadly effect in Russia, although they were also quite vulnerable, due to external fuel tanks.

Over 2,000 PzKpfw IIs were in service by May 1940, and, despite its obvious vulnerability, over 1,250 remained operational in January 1942. Initially it had been the backbone of the Panzer divisions, later it was relegated to reconnaissance tasks, there being five tanks allocated to each company, battalion and regimental headquarters. By May 1942, many of these tasks had been abolished and in 1943 it was axed completely, but was retained for other tasks, especially as Wespe.

On 15 March 1939, Czechoslovakia ceased to be a free and independent country, when Adolf Hitler annexed Bohemia and Moravia, incorporating them as a protectorate into the Third Reich. Slovakia remained, supposedly, independent, but was thereafter closely linked to Germany. All the arms and equipment which had belonged to the Czech Army was commandeered, while the thriving Czech armament industry came under German control. The Czechs had long held a world-wide reputation for producing high quality weapons, including tanks, which now found their way to the Wehrmacht. The PzKpfw 35(t) and PzKpfw 38(t) and their variants formed an important part of the Panzerwaffe.

MEDIUM TANKS

By the mid-1930s, German ideas on what tanks they needed to equip their burgeoning Panzer divisions, were beginning to crystallise. Initially it had been felt that they could manage with just two types of tanks, one light, fast and armed with a 2cm gun, while the other was heavier, slower, but armed with a larger gun that would be capable of close support. The former was of course the PzKpfw II, the latter a medium-weight tank, that was initially known by the code name 'Medium Tractor' (*Mittleren Traktor*), then as the *Bataillonführerswagen* and eventually as

Below: **The PzKpfw III (Fl) flamethrower version, of which 100 were produced in early 1943. It used the same chassis as the Ausf M, but mounted a 14mm** *Flammenwerfer* **(range – just under 60m) instead of the 50mm main gun.** *(TM)*

Right: **The PzKpfw III** *Artillerie-Panzerbeobach-tungwagen* **(armoured artillery OP) used a gun tank chassis without turret armament – the dummy gun and centrally-placed machine gun were mounted on a thicker mantlet, the lower MG was also removed.** *(TM)*

PzKpfw IV. However, experience with PzKpfw I & II rapidly convinced the Germans that they needed yet another type of tank, somewhere between the two types in weight, and armed with a more powerful gun than the PzKpfw II, which had to be capable of penetrating most types of enemy armour. General Guderian and his new Armoured Troops Command, wanted this tank to mount at least a 5cm anti-armour gun, but the Heereswaffenamt opted for a 3.7cm on the grounds of standardisation with the main infantry anti-tank gun of the period. Fortunately, Guderian was both forceful and far-sighted enough to get them to agree that the turret ring

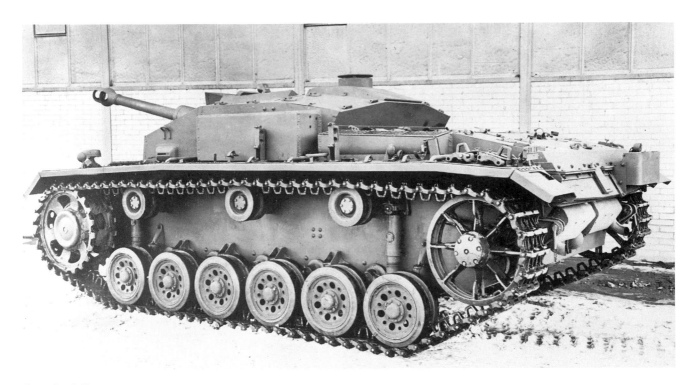

Above: **StuG 40 Ausf F which entered service in 1942. The longer 75mm StuK gun could defeat both T-34 and KV-1.** *(TM)*

Far left below: **This modified version of the VK2001 (Rh), built by Rheinmetall Borsig AG in 1935, was a direct successor to the *Bataillonführerswagen*. Also it was the predecessor to the PzKpfw IV series, which became the backbone of the Panzerwaffe, remaining in production from 1935 until March 1945.** *(TM)*

should be of sufficient diameter so as to be capable of accepting a larger weapon. Thus, the *Zugführerswagen* (platoon commander's vehicle) – later becoming known as the PzKpfw III (SdKfz 141) – was born. Its size, shape and layout were all very similar to the heavier PzKpfw IV. Both would have five-man crews, three in the turret and two in the hull, with the commander in his own raised position within the turret and equipped with all-round vision devices, while all members of the crew would be able to converse through an intercom, a standard part of the tank's radio equipment.

Development contracts were issued for the tank in 1935 and various prototypes were tested the following year. The Daimler Benz design was then

Left: **Three of the five-man crew of this PzKpfw IV Ausf D are visible, there remains just the driver and gunner inside. The vehicle number ends in 1, denoting it as the company commander's tank.** (TM)

selected and the first production model, the Ausf A, was running in 1936. Ten Ausf A (at the time called the 1/ZW) were built by Daimler Benz, between 1936 and 1937. Main armament was the 3.7cm KwK L/46.5 gun, with two co-axially mounted MG 34 in the turret; a third in the hull was manned by the radio operator. Powered by the V-12 Maybach HL 108TR petrol engine the 15.4 ton tank achieved a top speed of 20mph. The suspension had five large double bogie wheels on either side, mounted on coil-springs, with a front mounted sprocket, rear idler and two return rollers. Armour was thin (15mm or less) and the tank was quickly found to be unsatisfactory and withdrawn from combat units in early 1940. Daimler Benz also built a small number of the Ausf B (2/ZW),

Below: **StuG III Ausf G, with 'Saukopf' (Pigs head) gun mantlet, entered battlefield service in late 1943.** (TM)

Above: **In company with Allied Honeys and Grants in this Desert tank park is a captured PzKpfw IV Ausf F 2, the first type of PzKpfw IV to mount the long-barrelled 75mm gun. Note the early single-baffle muzzle brake.** *(TM)*

Right: **A brand-new PzKpfw IV Ausf E, still at the factory. Shown clearly are the new simplified driving sprocket and pivoting driver's visor.** *(TM)*

which was similar to the Ausf A, but with a suspension system which comprised eight small bogie wheels on each side, mounted in pairs and supported by leaf springs. It was also withdrawn from operational service in 1940 and was followed by two further short runs of models Ausf C (3a/ZW), and Ausf D (3b/ZW), both with improved suspensions, but both of which suffered

the same fate, being withdrawn from operational service after the Polish campaign.

Ausf E (4/ZW) was the first PzKpfw III to go into extended production (just under 100 built), principally because the designers had at last managed to get the suspension right – the six individual torsion-bar supported road wheels became standard for the tank, which now had frontal armour 30mm

Above: **This up-gunned PzKpfw IV Ausf D is fitted with a 75mm KwK L/48 gun and also additional spaced armour around the sides of the turret.**
(TM)

Left: **The PzKpfw IV Ausf G was very like the F2 version, with the long-barrelled 75mm gun, but with slightly thicker side armour. On the side rack are the excellent 'Jerricans', which held 20 litres (4 ½ gallons). These were far superior to the British thin tin petrol cans.**
(TM)

thick, weighed 19.5 tons and was 16ft 6ins long, 6ft 6ins high and 9ft 9ins wide. In September 1939, it was announced that the PzKpfw III had been chosen after successful troop trials, however, at about the same time it was realised that Guderian had been right all along and that the 3.7cm gun was not powerful enough. Unfortunately, production of a new gun would take time, so the Ausf F, which began production in September 1939, still fitted the 3.7cm gun, the 5cm gun not being available until the last quarter of the production run (total build for the Ausf F was 435). Over 1,200 Ausf Gs were ordered initially, but the windfall of PzKpfw 38(t) from Czechoslovakia, reduced this number to 600, almost all of which mounted the 5cm KwK L/42 gun. The gun performance was better, although the

Far left: **GIs advancing through the ruins of Pontfarcy on the Brest Penninsula, France, pass an abandoned PzKpfw IV Ausf H. More of this model were produced than any other PzKpfw IV (over 3,700).** *(TM)*

Left: **A PzKpfw Ausf H being inspected by a German tank crew. It appears to have been coated, even on the track guards, with** *Zimmerit* **anti-magnetic paste.** *(TM)*

muzzle velocity was slightly lower - 2250fps instead of 2445fps - the projectile weight was trebled to 4.5lb against of 1.5lb, while penetration, using APC, was almost doubled from 30mm to 56mm at 500 metres. Other improvements were also incorporated, the Ausf H having a newly-designed turret, transmission and running gear. Also it had an additional 30mm of add-on armour to the front plate, making it impossible for the contemporary Allied tank guns to knock it out at normal engagement range.

This add-on armour was incorporated onto the next model – Ausf J – of which more were built than any other in the PzKpfw III series. A total of 2,616 being produced between March 1941 and July 1942. In addition, the last 1,000 of this model were fitted (on Hitler's personal orders) with the new longer-barrelled L/60 gun, giving added muzzle velocity and an improved armour piercing performance. The tank also now had thicker armour (up to 50mm) as standard, a better visor for the driver and a new ball-mounting for the MG 34 in the hull. Further models (K, L & M) were all attempts at improving its protection, but it had become increasingly clear early 1943, when the final model, the Ausf N, went into production, that the tank was falling behind the standard of some of its opponents. It was therefore relegated to the close support role and, as we shall see, the

PzKpfw IV took its place as the main battle tank of the Panzer divisions, . The Ausf N was fitted with the 7.5cm KwK L/24 short-barrelled gun, which was only 24 calibres in length, as opposed to the the 60 calibres of the long-barrelled 'Special' 5cm gun. It fired a heavier projectile more suited in the close-support role.

A total of 15,350 ZW chassis were produced between 1939 and 1945, which is positive evidence of its value to the Panzerwaffe. The tank was used in

Above: **This PzKpfw IV Ausf G was captured in Normandy, July 1944. In darkness and under heavy mortar fire, a REME section managed to bring it back intact to their Brigade workshop.** *(TM)*

action on all fronts from Poland onwards, rapidly becoming the main weapon of the Panzer divisions, owing to the vulnerability of the lighter Is and IIs, together with the continuing use of the IV as an infantry support tank. Undoubtedly the long-barrelled 'Specials' were treated with respect by the Allies, especially when they were first used in combat in Russia and North Africa.

Among the most interesting variants was the *Tauchpanzer III* (diving tank), originally designed for the invasion of England – Operation Sealion.

The diving tank was a converted Ausf F, G, H or the *Befelswagen*, with all the external openings protected by a special sealant making them watertight. The gap between the hull and turret was closed by means of an inflatable rubber gland, while waterproof covers shrouded the cupola, gun mantlet and hull MG. Under the water, the engine drew its air through two tall tailpipes, fitted with non-return valves and could operate in depths up to 15metres remaining submerged for about 20 minutes. When Sealion was cancelled, most of the 168 *Tauchpanzer*

L/24 gun was chosen. It was decided to mount the gun direct onto the hull, dispensing with any form of turret and thus lowering the silhouette - compare the 8ft height of the PzKpfw III Ausf F, with the 6ft 5ins height of the StuG III. Despite not having a turret its weight was considerable - 19.6 tons, due to the fact that the frontal armour was extremely thick. The StuG III Ausf A, built in 1940, had a four-man crew, a top speed of 25mph, and a 100 miles range. In September 1941, on Hitler's personal orders, StuG III was up-armoured and up-gunned by fitting the 7.5cm StuK longer barrelled gun. It continued in service for the rest of the war, as did the final model, the Ausf G, which had a partially cast superstructure and mantlet which was called '*Saukopf*' by its crews, as it resembled a pig's head! Variants included an assault howitzer, mounting a 10.5cm StuH 42 L/28, a flamethrower and an ammunition carrier. Total build of StuG IIIs was over 9,000 (including 1,200 StuH). Significantly, the gallant Michael Wittmann, Germany's top tank ace, learned his skills as the commander of one of the first StuG III (allocated to the Leibstandarte SS Adolf Hitler) knocking out many enemy tanks on the Eastern Front - six in one battle!

If any single tank qualified for the title: 'Backbone of the Panzer Divisions' then it was undoubtedly the PzKpfw IV, which began life as the medium tractor (*Mittleren Traktor*), later changed

Left: **Russian soldiers riding on a captured PzKpfw IV Ausf H.** (TM)

Below: **This immaculate PzKpfw IV Ausf G is in the Panzermuseum at Munster Ortze, Germany. It was captured by the British, near Tobruk on 21 October 1942, from 8th Panzer Regiment of 15th Panzer Division and taken to Britain the following month. In 1960, it was returned to the Panzermuseum in exchange for a** *Spahpanzerluchs.*

were modified for use in river crossings by means of fitting a schnorkel pipe to the commander's cupola. These were used to great effect, crossing the River Bug at the start of Operation Barbarossa.

Variants included a flamethrower, a command tank, assault gun/tank destroyer, an ARV, and more. The *SturmGeschutz* assault gun/TD proved to be the most successful destroying more enemy armour than did the PzKpfw III gun tank. The decision to develop a special dual purpose armoured assault gun/TD was made in June 1936 and the 7.5cm

to *Bataillonführerswagen* (BW). The general designation was agreed in January 1934, that it would be a close-support medium tank, with a short-barrelled 7.5cm gun as its main armament, weigh under 24 tons, with layout, armour thickness, and other detail as for the PzKpfw III. Rheinmetall-Borsig AG produced a wooden mock-up (VK2001(Rh)) with the first prototype being built in 1935 of mild steel and weighing around 18tons. Two other prototypes were built, one each, by Krupp AG and MAN with all three being trialled at the Kümmersdorf testing grounds. The Krupp model (VK2001(K)) was chosen and the first production model 1/BW appeared in 1936. The initial order was for thirty-five which were all completed by March 1938.

The Ausf A (18ft 4ins long, 8ft 7ins high and 9ft 6ins wide) really set the pattern for the first few models of the tank, instantly recognisable by its suspension which comprised four bogies on each side, each carrying a pair of rubber-tyred roadwheels with quarter elliptical leaf springs, front drive sprocket, rear idler and four top rollers. It remained virtually unaltered throughout its long career, as did the drum shaped commander's cupola with its eight vision slits located towards the back of the turret. The next three models incorporated a number of improvements, the most significant being fitting the Ausf B with the more powerful 320hp Maybach HL120TR engine and the new SSG 76, six-speed gearbox. After the Ausf D had been given a thorough testing the requisite Army Regulation (No 685 dated 27 September 1939) was published and stated that the tank was declared ready in every way for service. Over 220 Ausf Ds were produced in total, but only a handful had been completed before war was declared, however, battle experience in Poland showed that the armour was too thin and had to be improved by attaching plates to the front and sides. The next model, the Ausf E, had increased basic protection - up to 50mm on the front glacis, plus extra 20mm plate bolted to the hull and superstructure sides.

The next major change came with the exchange of roles between PzKpfw III and IV, in the case of the latter it was during the production of Ausf F. The first 462 produced between April 1941 and March 1942 mounted the short 7.5cm KwK37L/24 gun, while the remaining 175, together with a few conversions, were armed with the long-barrelled KwK40/L43 (again on Hitler's personal orders). Ammunition stowage was altered to cope with the larger rounds and in fact more (87 instead of 80) were stowed. The muzzle velocity of the new gun was 2,428fps as opposed to 1,263fps, almost doubling its performance at a stroke, as the following figures show:

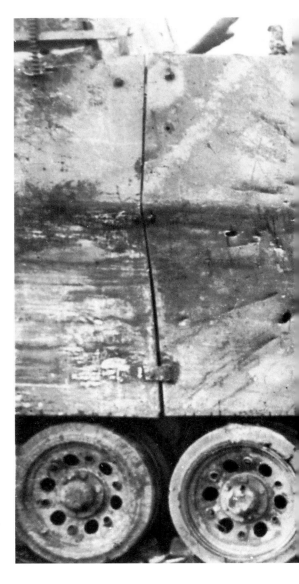

Type of 7.5cm fitted and type of ammunition used		Penetration in mm at range in yards			
		500	1000	1500	2000
KwK37 short -	APCBC	46	41	35	
	HEAT	43	43	43	43
KwK40 long -	APCBC	84	72	62	53

From Ausf A to Ausf F2 some 1,300 PzKpfw IV had been built in total: the Ausf G would more than double that production figure, 1,600 plus being built between May 1942 and June 1943. Various modifications in this long production run included the fitting of the improved KwKL/48 gun which gave a significantly better anti-armour performance and additional add-on armour (including for the first time thin steel side plates for production against such weapons as the Bazooka). The tank was now 21ft 8ins long, 8ft 9ins high and 9ft 6ins wide. The Ausf H was built in even greater numbers – nearly 4,000 chassis being produced, although not all were used for gun tanks. Thicker armour (now up to 80mm on the front glacis), the new SSG 77 gearbox and other modifications – increased all up weight to 25 tons and resulted in a slight drop in performance. The final production model, the Ausf J, followed, over 1,700 being built by March 1945, bringing the total of PzKpfw IV produced to over 8,500, representing over one-third of Germany's total wartime tank production. This last model had the electric powered turret traverse removed to save weight and a greater fuel capacity, both of which combined to give an increase in range to 200 miles.

Left: **A graphic impression of a strike on the bazooka protection plates of this StuG 40.** *(TM)*

Left: **Sturmpanzer IV** *Brummbär* **(Grizzly Bear), 150mm assault howitzer on a PzKpfw IV chassis. Just under 300 were produced and rushed to t he Eastern front to take part in the Kursk offensive in 1943.** *(TM)*

Right: **A Tauchpanzer IV** towing a field-manufactured fuel trailer in the early days of Barbarossa. The submersible PzKpfw IV was one of the 42 converted in late 1940, and used in the crossing of the River Bug on 22 June 1941, at the start of the invasion of the Soviet Union. They were fully sealed with an inflatable rubber gland around the turret ring, waterproof fabric seals on mantlet, cupola and with non-return valves on the exhausts. The fuel trailer was necessary after the Russian 'scorched earth' policy prevented the Germans from acquiring local fuel as they had managed to in the Low Countries and France in May 1940. *(TM)*

PzKpfw IV first saw battle service in Poland, where, despite the small numbers involved, it did so well that Guderian singled it out for special praise, commenting that it should be produced in much larger numbers than had been previously proposed. When the assault on the West began only 278 were available for combat out of a tank force of some 2,574. The 'Specials' more than held their own for most of the war, even against T-34 and KV 1, which were, in most respects, better than anything the Germans could produce until Tiger and Panther entered service.

Forty PzKpfw IV Ausf D & E were converted to *Tauchpanzers* and all were issued to eighteen Panzer regiments for the crossing of the River Bug. Twenty Ausf C & D chassis were converted to bridgelayers (*Bruckenleger IV*). Others were converted infantry assault bridges (*Infanterie*

Sturmsteg) or to *Bergepanzer* repair and recovery vehicles, while some became ammunition and stores or carriers, command and OP vehicles. They had a wide variety of guns fitted, including AA, SP guns, howitzers. The most well known of these being StuG IV, JagdPz IV, Hummel and Brummbar. There were five types of tank destroyer with 3,600 in total built, all of which were very effective, despite the fact that the most heavily armed Hornisse/Nashorn (Hornet/Rhino) was top heavy and difficult to steer on rough terrain.

Name	Armament	Superstructure on PzKpfw IV	No. produced/converted
StuG IV	7.5cm StuK 40L/48	StuG III	1,100+
JgdPz IV	7.5cm PaK 9 L/48	Improved StuG III	800 approx
Pz IV/ 70(V)	7.5cm PaK 42 L/70	Improved JgdPz IV	Vomag version over 900
Pz IV/ 70(A)	ditto	ditto	Alkett version 300 approx
Nashorn	8.8cm PaK 43/1 L/71	lengthened hull	500

Note: PaK (Panzer abwehr Kanone)

MEDIUM HEAVY & HEAVY TANKS

Although the PzKpfw III & IV were better than the vast majority of Russian tanks opposing the Panzer divisions during the invasion of Russia on 22 June 1941, the Germans soon had to face both a superlative new medium tank the T-34 and a very good new heavy tank, KV1 – both being better armed and better protected than anything in service in the Panzerwaffe. German confidence was shaken by these two new tanks, especially the T 34, as it had always been assumed that they could produce better AFVs than the Russians and could not believe that they had lost their superiority quite so quickly. In 1939, 1940 and 1941, victory had followed victory without any hitches, so no serious plans had been made to replace PzKpfw III & IV, although a 30-ton tank (VK3001(H)) had been contemplated much earlier. The 65 ton, 'Breakthrough Tank' (*Durchbruchswagen*) (VK 6501(H)) was still under test at Sennelager. Having realised the seriousness of the situation the Heereswaffenamt was swift to take remedial action, a team of experts being sent out to Russia immediately to make an on the spot examination of the problem. The team, which was composed of experts from the Army Ordnance Office, the armaments industry, tank designers and tank building firms, arrived at the 2nd Panzer Army front on 20 November 1941, to examine captured T-34s, and to discuss with Panzer crewmen their relevant battle experience. Some clearly felt that the best answer would be merely to ship a T-34 home and to copy it bolt for bolt. However, that was never the German way, and instead a new specification was issued by the Heereswaffenamt to MAN and Daimler-Benz for an entirely new medium to heavy

Below left: **The PzKpfw IV-based *Bruckenleger* (bridgelayer) carried a 29ft 3in Magirus bridge which was laid by using a forward pivoting gantry . Only 20 were built in 1940 after which it was cancelled and most were converted back to gun tanks.** *(TM)*

Below: **PzKpfw V Ausf G, a late model Panther, was produced between March 1944 and April 1945. It has the modified gun mantlet and better vision devices.** *(TM)*

Above: **The Jagdpanther was probably the best tank destroyer of the war. Its 88mm gun, low silhouette (only 9ft high) and powerful engine (top speed nearly 30mph) made it widely feared on the battlefield. Less than 400 were built.** *(TM)*

Right: **The Bergepanther was an excellent armoured recovery vehicle, capable of towing heavy tanks. Some 340 were produced and a small number converted from gun tanks. This one is on test by REME in Britain.** *(TM)*

tank - Project VK 3002, following basic guidelines: weight - 30 to 35 tons; armour (min.) - 60mm on the front, 40mm on the sides and rear; top speed - 25-35mph; armament arrangement - similar to T-34; main weapon - 7.5cm L/48 gun. Both firms produced their proposals in record time despite the fact that they had to incorporate a steady stream of modifications, the most important being the requirement to incorporate the newly-designed and more powerful L/70 gun.

The Daimler Benz proposal weighed about 34 tons, was powered by a diesel engine and looked very like T-34, while MAN's offering was much more a conventional German tank of the period. Hitler initially favoured the Daimler Benz design although he felt it should have a bigger gun. This directly led to an order being placed for 200 VK 3002(DB). However, the Panther Committee preferred the MAN design and, surprisingly, Hitler gave way to them. The MAN design was chosen, the DB order conveniently shelved, and production commenced. Initially it was planned to produce 250 a month but at the end of 1942 this was increased to 600 a month, so manufacture had to be arranged with other firms, including Daimler Benz!

In mid-July 1941, Rheinmetall-Borsig was awarded a contract to develop a gun capable of penetrating 140mm of armour plate at 1,000 metres.

At the same time they were contracted to design a turret for the VK 3002 project which would house the new L/70 gun. They met their target dates on both contracts and the gun entered full production, initially with a single muzzle brake, but later with a double-baffle. It was a remarkable weapon with a superlative performance as the following figures show: Muzzle Velocity: 3070fps. Ammunition: APCBC, 15lb shell. Penetration of homogeneous armour plate at 30 degrees – 141mm at 500 metres range; 121mm at 1000 metres range; 88mm at 2000

Top: **Panther V Ausf A** *Panzer-befelswagen.* **The command version of Panther.**

Above: **The impact of the Russian T-34 on the German Panzers, led to the rapid design and building of Panther.** *(GF)*

metres range – this was significantly better than that of the 88mm mounted on Tiger I.

Panther, as the new tank was named, first rolled off the production line at MAN in November 1942. The first model was initially known as the Ausf A, although this was later changed to Ausf D. Development was undoubtedly rushed and this led to many problems, such as transmission and steering faults, because the parts were designed for use on lighter less powerful AFVs. Even the engine was prone to overheating. Everyone was worried, Guderian writing in his diary for example, that he had... 'spent 15 June worrying about our problem child, the Panther; the track, suspension and drive were not right and the optics were also not yet satisfactory'. The gun, however, lived up to its expectations according to one battlefield trials report, knocking out a T-34 with the first round at an unbelievable range of 7,224metres! The same report did not, however, make entirely satisfactory reading: of the 200 Panthers involved in this trial in Russia, 160 were out of action by the end of the first day and nine days later, there were only 43 serviceable. Many had broken down between the railhead and the battlefront and because of their

weight towing was extremely difficult. Eventually, these mechanical problems were cured and Panther gained a reputation for all-round excellence, just under 6,000 gun tanks being built, with many other variants using the same chassis.

PzKpfw V Models			
Mark	Ausf D	Ausf A	Ausf G
Weight (tons)	43	44.8	45.5
Dimensions			
Length all	29ft 1in		
Height	9ft 9ins	9ft 10ins	9ft 10ins
Width	11ft 3ins	11ft 2ins	11ft 1in
Crew all	five		
Main armament all	KwK42 L/70 gun		
Secondary	two MG 34		
Armour	16-100mm	16-110mm	16-110mm
Engine all	Maybach HL230P30		
Max Speed all	29mph		
Range all	125 miles		

Further development followed the Ausf D, the next model being called Ausf A – instead of Ausf E as might have been expected – first appearing in August 1943 with 1,788 built. It had an improved

Above: **This PzKpfw VI was captured in Tunisia, April 1943 and eventually brought back to Britain. It is currently being completely overhauled at the Tank Museum, Bovington.** *(TM)*

Left: **VK 4501, known also as Tiger (P), photographed at the Nibelungwerke factory - the man in the black hat is Dr Ferdinand Porsche who was responsible for many of the best aspects of German AFV turret design.**

Right: **Photographed on the 15th Panzer Division training area in Sagan, Silesia this excellent view of a Panther Ausf D, shows all the power and grace of this superb tank. The 75mm KwK 42 L/70 gun was extremely lethal, being able to penetrate 88mm of armour plate at 2000 metres.** *(TM)*

cupola for the commander, a new ball-mounting for the hull machine gun and better sighting equipment for the gunner (the TZF 12A monocular telescope replacing the older TZF 12 binocular telescope). A short-barrelled grenade projector which could fire both HE and smoke grenades was fitted in the turret roof, plus a roof-mounted periscope for the loader. The final production model, the Ausf G was built between March 1944 and April 1945 (3,740 in total) – it had a more sloping, thicker-sided hull, one piece side-plates, a strengthened front glacis (driver's vision port removed and replaced by a rotating periscope in the top of his compartment. Ammunition stowage was increased from 79 to 82 rounds.

Panther entered battlefield service in the Kursk region of Russia in July 1943 and afterwards was used everywhere – Italy, north west Europe and the Eastern Front, usually in partnership with PzKpfw IV to protect its flanks. The largest concentration of Panthers was assembled for the Ardennes offensive in December 1944, but there were never enough Panthers to meet requirements.

Command and artillery OP versions of Panther were produced. The ARV Bergepanther, was developed as it was impossible to recover Panther or Tiger easily with the standard halftrack recovery tractor. Stories abound of having to use halftracks in pairs, even three together, to move these heavy tanks. While only a handful of Tigers were ever converted, 350 of the very useful and effective Bergepanther were produced.

Having learned their lesson, German tank designers were never allowed to rest on their laurels for very long. Almost as soon as Panther production began, the Heereswaffenamt commissioned MAN and Henschel to look into new designs for an improved Panther, indeed, they were also told to look into Tiger designs and try to achieve as much standardisation as possible between the two tanks, so as to simplify manufacture, training, maintenance and repair. This resulted in Panther II and Tiger II. The former never got further than the prototype stage, whereas the latter did enter operational service. Panther II was overtaken by the E 50 project, a design to replace both Panther I and II. However, the design was not completed by the end of the war. In 1945, Daimler Benz produced a small number of prototype hulls for Panther Ausf F, the supposed successor to the Ausf G, the major change being the *Schmalturm* (small turret), but this project was also too late.

Probably the most important variant was the Jagdpanther, the best tank destroyer built by any nation during World War Two. Numerous SP guns, assault guns and TDs were already in service, built on other chassis, but all were to be overshadowed by Jagdpanther. Weighing 46 tonnes, it mounted the formidable 8.8cm FlaK gun (*Flieger abwehr Kanone*),

which was already being used with devastating results as a towed anti-tank gun. Almost 400 were built between January 1944 and the end of the war, the first entering service in June 1944.

In 1933-34, following a trend set by France with the *Char de Rupture* and Britain with the Independent, Germany had also produced a multi-turreted tank known as the *Neubaufahrzeug* (Nbz). Two prototypes and three experimental tanks were constructed, one version of which mounted two guns: a 7.5cm and 3.7cm (side-by-side) in the main turret, plus three machine guns (two of which were in smaller separate turrets front and rear). The Nbz was also, but probably only for propaganda purposes, called the PzKpfw VI, but nothing on common with Tiger. Instead, Tiger owes its origins firstly to the work being carried out on VK6501 and VK3001, and secondly, to Hitler's direct involvement in tank development. He personally ordered the design and building of a 36-ton tank (VK 3601). Both the VK3001 and VK3601 were cancelled in order to concentrate all effort on a new project, the VK4501, which was

designed to mount a version of the highly successful 8.8cm FlaK 36 gun. Hitler favoured the use of this gun, which had already proved itself in the anti-tank role. The Heereswaffenamt preferred the fitting of a lighter gun in order to keep the vehicle's overall weight down, so while Krupp designed a turret for the 8.8cm, Rheinmetall developed a lighter one for the KwKL/70 gun. When the order for the new tank had been placed in May 1941, the companies had been informed that the prototypes were to be ready for testing on the Führer's birthday - 20 April 1942. Porsche and Henschel both had to cut corners, by incorporating the best features of their previous designs VK 3001 and VK 3601, to meet the production deadlines for their prototypes VK 4501(P) and VK 4501(H) respectively. Dr Ferdinand Porsche was a personal favourite of the Führer, but the Henschel model was so clearly the superior of the two tanks at this and subsequent trials, that it was chosen. Porsche were so confident of their design winning that they already started a production run of their Tiger (P). The Tiger (P)s

Above left: **British soldiers inspecting a Tiger after its capture on the Djebel Djaffa.** *(TM)*

Above: **Using Schnorkel equipment as seen fitted here, Tiger I could travel under water to a maximum depth of thirteen feet.** *(TM)*

Left: **Tiger II was the most powerful tank used in World War Two. The 88mm KwK 43 L/71 gun could penetrate 127mm of armour at a range of 2300 metres.** *(TM)*

Above: **Another immaculate tank from the Panzermuseum in Germany. This is the Tiger II, the production model with the Henschel turret.**

Above right: **Tiger II fitted with the streamlined, but more vulnerable Porsche turret (due to the shot trap). The first 50 had this turret, from then on production tanks had Henschel turrets.** *(TM)*

Right: **Tigermörser mounted a 38cm heavy assault mortar on the Tiger I chassis. Eighteen Tiger I were converted in the latter half of 1944.** *(TM)*

built were not wasted although they never entered service as gun tanks, being modified as heavy tank destroyers, mounting the 8.8cm PaK 43/2, L/71 anti-tank gun in a large fixed turret at the rear of the chassis. They were named Ferdinand (after Dr Porsche?) and later re-named Elephant.

PzKpfw VI Ausf E	
Date of origin	1942
Weight (tons)	57
Crew	five
Dimensions	
Length	27ft 8ins
Height	9ft 7ins
Width	12ft 1in
Armament	8.8cm KwK36 L/56 and two MG 34
Armour	25-100mm
Max speed	23.75 mph
Range	140 miles

Henschel commenced production in July 1942 and over the next two years, up to August 1944, built a total of 1,354 Tiger I. There were no actual different models, although some improvements were introduced throughout the production run. Nevertheless, it had a number of different nomenclatures, including Ausf H, Ausf E, Tiger E or Tiger I, but no matter what it was called, just a glimpse of its instantly recognisable shape was enough to make Allied tank commanders blood run cold. Its reputation was of course exaggerated,

but from the moment it appeared on the battlefield in the Leningrad area in August 1942, its place in history was assured, despite the fact that it was rushed into battle in small numbers on unsuitable terrain – a classic example of Hitler's impatience. Only four Tigers were used on very soft going and all suffered mechanical failures, but were recovered and repaired, only to be committed again over equally soft ground with even more disastrous results. Major Richard Maerker who had been commanding the Tigers was made the scapegoat for Hitler's stupidity, despite the fact that he had made protest after protest about the state of the ground. Next time it would be a very different story: four Tigers were sent to assist the 96th Infantry Division, which was being overrun by twenty-four T-34 tanks. In a sharp exchange of fire the Tigers quickly knocked out a twelve T-34 while the rest turned and retreated. The Tiger's reputation was of course greatly enhanced by such brilliant tank commanders as SS Hauptsturmführer Michael Wittmann, who won his Knight's Cross, Oakleaves and Swords, all within the space of five months. His exploits are legendary and include delaying the entire 7th Armoured Division at Villers Bocage, and destroying its complete vanguard with just three Tigers and one PzKpfw IV under his command.

As with most other tanks, there were a small number, modified as command (*Befelswagen*) and

fitters (*Bergepanzer*) Tigers. Another version was a large 65-ton heavy assault mortar (*Sturmörser-Tiger*) a total of less than twenty of these vehicles were built.

As the war progressed and Germany was forced more and more onto the defensive, the need for fast-moving mobile forces lessened and the requirement was more for slower, better protected and better armed AFVs. After the T-34 débâcle, Hitler and his beloved Panzerwaffe were determined not to be unprepared again, the result being the heaviest and largest tank to see combat during World War Two, namely the Tiger II,

PzKpfw VI Ausf B (SdKfz 182), also called the *Königstiger* (King Tiger or Royal Tiger). Less than 500 of these beautiful, streamlined monsters were built by Henschel in the period January 1944 to March 1945. Designed from the outset to mount the new long-barrelled 8.8cm L/71 gun, two companies had originally been invited to submit designs - Henschel and Porsche, the latter merely revamping VK 4501(P), their Tiger (P) prototype, and producing a heavier version. However, this was rejected in favour of a second design VK 4502(P), which had a larger turret set back on the hull with a forward mounted engine

Weighing 68.43 tons (Porshe turret), 69.75 tons (Henschel turret), 33ft 9ins long, 10ft 1in high and 12ft 4ins wide, the Tiger II was an awesome machine. Its 700hp Maybach HL230P30 engine (as used in late production Panther Ausf Gs), allowed it on good going a maximum speed of around 20mph, but the power to weight ratio was much lower than both Panther and Tiger I making it difficult to manoeuvre, whilst cross-country fuel consumption was a staggering 2.48 gallons per mile! However, this was more than made up for by the L/71 gun, (probably the best all-round tank gun of World War Two) which could penetrate 215mm of armour at a range of 1000metres and 80mm of armour at a staggering range of 4000 metres. Tiger II first saw action on the Eastern Front in May 1944 and was deployed in Normandy and the Ardennes. Although always outnumbered, they could normally eliminate their enemy with ease.

A few Tiger II were converted to command tanks and known as the PzBefWeg mit 8.8cm KwK43 L/71. This necessitated reducing ammunition stowage by 17 rounds to allow the installation of the extra radio equipment.

Jagdtiger was the limited traverse version of the Tiger II, which at 70 tons was the heaviest German AFV to go into service. Its 34ft 11ins long chassis was just under 9ft 10ins high to the top of its vast fixed turret which contained a massive 12.8cm PaK 44 L/55 gun (later models had the PaK 80 L/55) although, due to a shortage of 12.8cm guns, some had to be fitted with the Jagdtiger's 8.8cm. Although 150 Jagdtigers were ordered, only seventy-seven were built in the period July 1944 to March 1945. First battle action was in the Ardennes, then later in the defence of Germany. The gun performance was better even than the L/71. With armour plate up to a maximum thickness of 250mm, the Jagdtiger was an incredible machine, but, like Tiger II, was underpowered and difficult to manoeuvre - the same engine being used as in the Panther.

SUPER HEAVY TANKS

One might have thought that the 69-ton Tiger II and 70-ton Jagdtiger were powerful enough to tackle anything on the battlefield, but that would be to discount the Führer's obsession with larger and larger tanks, which led to the building of two other monsters - the E100 at 140 tons and Maus, which weighed a massive 188 tonnes! Both never proceeded further than prototype stage, however the amount of industrial effort which both projects absorbed was considerable, so perhaps they were of more benefit to the Allies than to the Germans. Nevertheless, both were considerable

and electric transmission. Unfortunately for Porsche this was also cancelled, because the sea blockade of Germany was so effective there was a desperate shortage of copper which the new electric transmission needed. Porsche had manufactured fifty turrets (more streamlined than the Henschel) and these were subsequently fitted to the early production Tiger II. The design eventually accepted was VK 4503(H), first ordered officially in January 1943 and appearing as a prototype nine months later, the delay caused by attempts at parts standardisation with the new Panther II design.

feats of engineering. The Heereswaffenamt ordered the E-100 from Adlerwerke at the same time as Porsche was developing Maus. Porsche had been ordered in 1942 by Hitler to ensure that Maus mounted both a 12.5cm and a 7.5cm gun, and have armour as thick as possible (up to 240mm on the gun mantlet). Two prototypes were built in 1943 and a production order placed for a further 150. This order was cancelled in October 1943, when nine Maus were under construction. It was always thought that the two prototypes had been destroyed at the Kummersdorf test ground, but one survived and is displayed in the Russian Tank Museum at Kubinka, near Moscow.

The E-100 heavy tank was just one of a series of entirely new AFVs which the Germans had initiated in 1943, these covered six classes - E5 light tank, E10 light TD, E25 medium TD, E50 'light' battle tank to replace Panther, E75 'medium' battle tank to replace Tiger, and E-100

heavy tank. The E-100, which was to mount the same guns as Maus, was the furthest advanced of all the projects. In 1944 it was given the lowest possible priority, only three Adlerwerke employees were retained on the project, when Hitler momentarily came to his 'senses' and ordered a halt to all work on heavy tanks. At the time this included projects other than E-100 and Maus, one being VK7001(K) under which Krupp was studying a series of 100-170 ton superheavies, known as Tiger-Maus and Lion. Some consideration was also given to a 1,500 ton tank, to be powered by four submarine-type diesel engines, armour 250mm thick armed with two 11.5cm guns in rear-mounted turrets and an 8.8cm cannon at the front. Such a tank would have completed the full-circle back to the multi-turreted *Neubaufrzeug* of 1934, but fortunately for the German engineers at least, this project was cancelled and sanity prevailed!

CHAPTER FOUR

United States

Armor, as the ground arm of mobility, emerged from
World War Two with a lion's share of the credit for the allied victory.
Indeed armor enthusiasts regarded the tank as being the
main weapon of the land army.

US Army Lineage Series.

Although it had been Great Britain and France who had built and deployed more tanks than any other nation in World War One, the United States had undoubtedly embraced the armoured philosophy enthusiastically, forming the world's third largest tank force even though it was comprised, operationally, solely of British and French-built tanks. A few odd-looking contraptions were built by the US, including a steam tank and a skeleton tank, but in general terms American tank building did not begin until the production of the Ford 3 ton and 6 ton copies of the French Renault FT 17. None of these tanks saw action.

At the end of World War One, the US Tank Corps had just over 20,000 officers and men but by May 1919, it had been reduced to just 300 officers and 5,000 enlisted men manning three tank brigades, the Tank Center (with repair and depot companies) and the Tank Corps GHQ. A few months later, Congress fixed the size of the Corps at 154 officers and 2,508 men equipped with some 800 light and heavy tanks, the majority being Renault FT 17s and Ford-built copies.

Sadly, their days as an independent Corps were numbered being disbanded later in 1920, with all existing tank units assigned to the infantry. War Department policy also laid down that there would be only two types of tanks - Light (under 5 tons) and Medium (under 15 tons), the upper weight limits being imposed so that the Light could be carried on a truck, while the Medium could be

moved by rail and use existing road bridges and pontoons. The role of the tank became, as in the French Army, the close support for the infantry so tanks were distributed across the entire army, the considered view being that tanks were incapable of independent action. A further War Department policy statement of 1922 reiterated that the primary role of tanks was to: ... facilitate the uninterrupted advance of the infantryman in the attack.

To make matters worse, defence spending was cut to the absolute minimum making it impossible to maintain an effective tank army, so most of the best tank officers - men like Colonel George S. Patton Jr returned to the cavalry. Patton did maintain an interest in the tank and would return to fulfil his destiny, but that would not be until 1940.

Fortunately not everyone was entirely blinkered and in 1927, having witnessed the British Army's Experimental Mechanised Force exercising on Salisbury Plain, the Secretary of War, Dwight F. Davis ordered the US Army chief of Staff to set up a similar force. In 1928, the Experimental Mechanized Brigade assembled at Fort Meade. Unfortunately, this collection of worn-out, obsolete equipment soon earned the nickname: 'The Gasoline Brigade of rattle-trap trucks and aged tanks'. It was disbanded just two months later. Despite this abortive start, mechanization was inevitable and in 1930, the Mechanized Force returned, thanks in no small way to Brigadier General Adna A. Chaffee – the driving force and 'Father' of US armour. The

Cavalry had also begun to mechanize, however, as the infantry were the only service allowed to have tanks, their tanks had to be called Combat Cars. The Infantry Light Tank T2 was also used by the Cavalry, but they called it the Combat Car T1.

The dazzling success of the German Blitzkrieg in Poland galvanized America into action and the rapid conquest of the Low Countries then France finally convinced any sceptics. Only 325 light tanks had been built between 1939-40, to add to the handful of obsolete machines already in service, but by the end of the war US production was a staggering 88,410 tanks of all types. In most cases tank factories also had to be built before production could commence, a classic example was the Detroit Tank Arsenal; this not exist when Chrysler agreed to build the M3 medium tank. The steelwork of the factory was only erected by the end of 1940, yet by mid-April 1941 the first tank rolled off the assembly line! In three months production had increased to 100 tanks per month, the following year the Arsenal was enlarged and production increased to 700 tanks per month.

TANK PRODUCTION 1939-1945

	1939-40	1941	1942	1943	1944	1945	Total
light	325	2,591	10,947	8,212	4,043	2,801	28,919
medium	6	1,461	14,049	21,250	13,468	6,793	57,027
heavy	-	-	1	35	54	2,374	2,464
Total	331	4,052	24,997	29,497	17,565	11,968	88,410

Despite the US Army's massive expansion of its armored forces from two armored divisions in 1941 to a total of sixteen active divisions by the end of the war, together with some 65 non-division tank battalions (plus 29 in course of formation), not to mention tank destroyer battalions and amphibian tractor battalions, USMC tank units, etc, the Americans still built far more tanks than they needed. None were wasted, however, because they generously equipped many allied forces such as the Free French, Poles and South American countries such as Brazil, while they also supplied many tanks to their three major allies China, Great Britain (including the Commonwealth) and the Soviet Union. Such massive production was not without its problems, nevertheless, once American industry had satisfied the initial requirements for quantity they then turned their attention to standardization, improvements and efficiency generally but this did not always simplify matters. For example, at the end of 1942 there were five different models of the Sherman in production at the same time. 'We are beginning to run into the motor car dealer's problem,' commented the head of Chrysler's Ordnance Tank and Combat Vehicle Division in May 1942, 'Our customers, the fighting men, want only the latest models!'

Initially, when a tank was in its design and development stages it was known by a T number – for example, T26 was the Test stage number for the Pershing heavy tank. Any major modifications during this period were shown by adding an E

Above: **An M2A2 light tank being driven up a loading ramp on to a rail flatcar. The 'Mae West' is instantly recognisable by its two turrets, one mounting a .50 machine gun, the other a .30.** *(TM)*

Right: **Crashing over lines of wooden tank obstacles appears no problem to these M2A2's during a demonstration at Fort Benning, Georgia, early 1940.** *(TM)*

number, so T26E2 is the second experimental model of the T 26. These numbers were allocated chronologically. Once fully accepted into service the tank was no longer in the Test or Experimental stages, so it would be allocated an M number and to make everything more logical towards the end of hostilities, the M numbers were the same as the Ts, so the T 26 became the M26, but this was not always the case at the beginning of the war. Any major modification was shown by adding an A number (Sherman M4, M4A1, M4A2, M4A3 etc) and in some cases, the E suffix was also retained (M4A3E8 was the horizontal volute spring suspension (HVSS) version of this model).

Some tanks also were given an official names – such as Sherman, Grant and Lee, all being named after famous American generals.

LIGHT TANKS

In 1939, the US Army had four closely related light AFVs in service - the infantry had the Light Tanks M2A2 & M2A3, while the cavalry had Combat Cars M1 & M2. The simplest way of telling them apart was that the light tanks had twin turrets, so were nicknamed Mae Wests, for obvious anatomical reasons. The commander's turret

mounted a .50 heavy machine gun (HMG), in the other a .30 MG. Both turrets had limited traverse (270 degrees). The Combat Cars had a single turret with both MGs mounted coaxially, all had a third MG in the hull and another for AA defence. All had a crew of four, weighed around 9 tons (the twin-turreted tanks being slightly heavier) had the same armour thickness – 6.25mm to 15mm (except for M2A3 which had armour up to 17.5mm) and all were powered by the same seven-cylinder Continental W670-9A air-cooled radial engine. The combat cars had the better top speed (45mph instead of 30-40mph) and a longer range (140 instead of 130miles).

The last of the series to be constructed was the M2A4, which mounted a 37mm gun in a single, fully traversing turret with five .30 MGs (one co-ax, two in sponsons fired by the driver, one in the hull front and one AA on the commander's cupola). The 10.25-ton tank had a crew of four, armour up to 25mm thick and was powered by a slightly uprated Continental engine although in the last few production models it was replaced with a Guiberson T-1020 Series 4 diesel. First built in 1939 it had Cletrac double-controlled differential steering, vertical volute spring suspension (VVSS) and was 14ft 6ins long, 8ft 2ins high and 8ft 1¼ins wide. This was the first tank to be supplied to the British under Lend-Lease but was only used for training in Britain and the Middle East. Training was also their main role in the US. Total production was 375, being completed by April 1942.

The M2A4 was really the prototype for the next light tank series the M3, which was known as the Stuart I in British service and also earned itself the endearing nickname Honey from its crews on both sides of the Atlantic. Many of the features of the M2A4 were repeated, however, the major change was to improve its protection by thickening the armour (now 10-51mm) especially on the frontal area, removing vision ports on the sides of the turret and strengthening the engine decks. The weight increased by some 4,400lbs requiring stronger suspension to be fitted, this employed a trailing idler wheel thus increasing the contact between ground and track with better weight distribution.

Standardised in July 1940, the M3 went into production at the American Car & Foundry Company (ACF), who in the next two years, produced 5,811 (including 1,285 with diesel engines). Changes were made during this period, the seven-sided rivetted turret took on a rounded shape, the commander's cupola was removed thus reducing the tank's height. Welding replaced rivetting, as it offered better protection for the crew, in case rivet heads broke off when the tank was hit and became missiles inside the turret. Other improvements included dispensing with the two sponson MGs, fitting a power traverse and a gyrostabiliser (supposed to steady the gun while on the move, but this was found to be unreliable and was little used) also thicker armour. A new model, the M3A1 (Stuart II) was

Above: **The Cavalry Combat Car M1, shown had one turret instead of two as on the light tank. This example is from the 1st Cavalry Regiment of the 7th Cavalry Brigade, 1939.** *(TM)*

introduced in August 1941, which was followed by the M3A2 (Stuart III), the Stuart IV was the diesel-engined version of the M3A1. The final model which entered production in early 1943, was the M3A3 (Stuart V). It had an all-welded hull, sloping frontal armour and an improved radio compartment, it weighed almost 16 tons compared with a little over 14 tons for the M3A1. The small tank was declared obsolete by the US Army in July 1943, but remained in service all over the world. For example, in addition to the British Army, M3's were sent to the French in North Africa, the Soviet Union, Brazil and to China. The British first used the Stuart in action in the Western Desert, November 1941 and they were the first US tanks to see action against the Japanese.

M3A1 & A3 Production
M3A1   4,621 (including 211 diesels);
M3A3   3,427
(These figures and all others for M3 & M5 series are taken from 'Stuart, a history of the American light tank', by RP Hunnicutt).

Among the variants the most important were the M3 command tank, usually a field mod-ification, which had a welded box-like structure in place of the turret. The M3 and M3A1 flame-thrower on which the 37mm gun was replaced by a Satan flamegun (two minutes of sustained fire) and used in the Pacific. The Stuart Kangaroo, a British conversion of the M3 had the turret removed and seats added.

	M3	M5
Crew	four	four
Dimensions		
Length	14 ft 10¾ ins	14 ft 2¾ ins (15 ft 10½ ins M5A1)
Height	8 ft 3 ins	7 ft 6½ ins
Width	7 ft 4 ins	7 ft 4¼ ins
Weight	2.23tons	14.73tons (15.16tons M5A1)
Armour	10-51mm	12-67mm
Armament	37mm gun up to five MGs	37mm gun three MGs (co-ax, hull, AA)
Engine	250hp Continental or Guiberson diesel	twinV-8 Cadillac (110hp each)
Max speed	36mph	36mph
Range	70-90miles	100miles

In mid-1941, the Ordnance Department concerned about a shortage of Continental radial engines - which were also required by the ever-growing aircraft industry - decided to introduce diesel engines and a few M3 and M3A1s were, as

Left: **On parade in Washington, DC. This M2A4 is armed with a 37mm and co-ax .30 MG, plus two more MG's in the side sponsons, one MG in the hull front and fifth on an AA mounting on the turret.** *(TM)*

Above: **An M3A1 light tank being towed to a field repair base, during training in Britain, prior to D-Day. This version had an all- welded hull and turret.** *(TM)*

Right: **M5A1 light tank equipped for 'Psywar', with a loud hailer and public address equipment.** *(TM)*

already explained, powered by Guiberson diesels. However, it was clear that the need to change from air-cooled radials would become more pressing, so they requested the Cadillac Division of General Motors to build a prototype light tank which would be powered by twin V-8 Cadillac petrol engines and fitted with automatic transmission (a recent development in the car industry). Tests quickly proved that the engine was superior to all others (including radials), while in October 1941 a Cadillac-powered light tank drove 500 miles from Detroit to the Aberdeen Proving Ground (APG) in Maryland without a hitch. Subsequent testing at APG showed that the engines provided more power, ran more smoothly and were quieter. And, the biggest plus of all, they were immediately available in large numbers.

In the course of installing the new engine, Cadillac had made so many changes to the M3 that it was accepted as a new model which was originally called the M4, but this was changed to M5 so as not to cause confusion with the M4

Left: **The M3 in Canadian service, where it was known as the Stuart I. Note the side machine gun sponsons have been blanked off.** *(TM)*

Sherman. The M5 went into full production at the Cadillac factory in Detroit in March 1942, and later that year at their factory at Southgate, California and at the Massey-Harris Company plant, Racine, Wisconsin. In October 1943, ACF also switched their production from M3 to M5.

In September 1942, the M5A1 was standardised in order to bring the M5 series in line with all the

Above: **M3A1s of the Soviet Army fording a river in the Taman Penninsula, Eastern Front, 1943. The United States provided over 1, 600 M3A1s, on Lend-Lease to the Soviets.** *(TM)*

Right: **The M22 Locust light tank was used (being ferried in Hamilcar gliders) operationally by the British 6th Airborne Reconnaissance Regiment during the Rhine Crossing 24th March 1945.** *(TM)*

modifications now standard on the M3A3 which included a new turret (with a bulge at the rear for the radio), larger hatches for driver and co-driver, improved all-round vision devices, a better gun mount for the 37mm, dual traverse controls thus allowing the commander to traverse onto a target, detachable sand shields and a shield to protect the AA, MG (a very late modification). The M5A1 replaced the M5 on all production lines from early 1943, by which time some 2,074 M5s had been produced. A further 6,810 M5A1s were then built up to June 1944. Some 1,431 M5A1s were assigned to British service during 1943-44 and saw service in North West Europe, being given the designation: Stuart VI.

In addition to an M5 command tank, M5 dozer and the T8 reconnaissance vehicle all of which had their turrets removed before fitting a box-like structure, a dozer blade and a .50MG on a ring mounting, respectively, the most widely used variant was the Howitzer Motor Carriage (HMC) M8. This mounted a 75mm gun in an open-topped turret, 1,778 were built by Cadillac between September 1942 and January 1944.

Impressed by the successes of the German airborne forces, the United States began to look towards building a force of paratroopers, but quickly realised that without mobility and armoured

support their fighting potential would be severely limited. With this in mind, in February 1941 the Ordnance Board began design studies for a 7.5ton tank which could be air-transported and landed.

Several designs were proposed, the best being one by the Marmon-Herrington Company. A pilot model, designated the Light Tank T9 (Airborne) was approved in autumn 1941 and two

The original weight limit had to be increased with the agreement of the US Army Air Corps and the British, who were now also showing interest in the project. The T9E1 was completed in November 1942 and tested at APG, while a second pilot was sent to Britain for evaluation. In April 1942, the T9E1 was approved and even before proper standardisation, they started to roll off the assembly line. An order was placed for 1,900, but it was cancelled after only 830 had been built (April 1943 - February 1944). Extensive testing took place during 1943-44, including flight tests (in a C-54 aircraft) which resulted in certain modifications. Finally in August 1944, six months after production ceased, the T9E1 was standardised as the M22.

The British, who named it Locust, received 260 tanks and these saw operational service with the 6th Airborne Armoured Reconnaissance Regiment (AARR). The AARR, who had used the British Tetrach airborne tank during Operation Overlord and the Battle of the Bulge, were re-equipped with Locust for the Rhine Crossing. It suffered the fate of all small, light tanks, when faced with heavily armed opposition so the AARR soon handed over their Locusts in exchange for British Cromwells and then continued their advance. The major drawback of

Above: **T9E1 was the second pilot model of the T9 light tank and incorporated modifications to the original hull shape to improve protection. Standardised as the M22, 830 were built but were never used in combat by the US forces. However, a large number were supplied to the British.** *(TM)*

further pilot models were built in 1942. In essence the 7.3ton, T9 looked like a small Sherman (length: 13ft, width: 7ft 4½in, height: 6ft) with a crew of three, a 37mm gun plus three MG (one co-ax, two in the bow), a welded hull and armour 25mm thick. It was powered by a six-cylinder 162hp Lycoming air-cooled engine, which gave it a top speed of 40mph and a range of 135 miles.

Above: **The M3A3 had a larger, welded hull, allowing more room for larger fuel tanks and extra ammunition stowage. In British service it was known as Stuart V.** *(TM)*

Right: **An M5A1 equipped with a Culin hedgerow cutter.** *(TM)*

the M22 was definitely its thin armour (maximum 25mm) which could not keep out even .50 armour piercing (AP) ammunition. An interesting modification was the fitting of the Littlejohn Muzzle Adaptor to some of the M22s sent to Britain. This increased the muzzle velocity by squeezing the AP shot down by approximately one third. There were no variants except for a trial rebuild of a Locust into the T10 light tractor (airborne), intended to seat five men and tow a 105mm airborne howitzer, but the project was cancelled in 1943.

As the war progressed, it became clear that the M3 and M5 series were, like most other light tanks of all the combatants, lacking in firepower and protection to enable them to survive on the modern battlefield. Therefore, it was felt that a more powerful light tank was needed.

In early 1941, this was translated into a definite requirement for a 14-ton tank with a low silhouette, armour up to 38mm thick and mounting a 37mm gun. Two pilots were designed at the Rock Island Arsenal, the first T7 had a welded hull and a cast turret, the next T7E1 was of rivetted construction. The latter was never fully completed because rivetted armour was no longer favoured. However, the chassis, which had HVSS

suspension as opposed to VVSS, was used for transmission and suspension trials. The wooden mock-up of the T7 was followed by three prototypes T7E2, T7E3 & T7E4 built to test different engine, transmission and armour configurations. The T7E2 showed the most

potential. It had a cast hull and turret, the engine was a Wright R975 air-cooled radial.

While the tank was being built it was decided to up-gun it to 57mm, using a gun adapted from the British 6 pounder and due to be fitted to the Canadian Ram tank. Later, the Armored Force requested a 75mm gun to be fitted even though this meant re-designing the turret. Another major change was to increase the thickness of the armour to 63mm, increasing its weight up to 25 tons thus placing the T7 outside the light tank class and causing it to be reclassified as the M7 medium tank. It was standardized in August 1942 and an order placed for 3,000 with International Harvester, to begin production in December 1942. Fortunately, further testing took place and the pilot was found to be grossly underpowered because its fully equipped weight had now increased to 29 tons! Work began on re-engining the M7 just as the M4 Sherman started to roll off the assembly line, so the need for both was rightly queried and the M4 chosen as the better of the two. The M7 project was cancelled and later declared obsolete.

However, the Ordnance Board requirement for a better light tank remained and they contracted Cadillac, makers of the M5, to design a new tank which would incorporate all the best features of the T7/M7 project. They produced the T24, which had two 110hp Cadillac petrol engines, the automatic transmission of the M5 and a 75mm M6 main gun. A weight limit of 18 tons was put on the project, which meant that the tank's armour thickness would be 9 to 25mm (length: 16ft 4½ins, width: 9ft 4ins, height: 7ft 3ins) . The pilot T24 was completed in October 1943 and was so successful that authorisation was given immediately for 1,000 to be built, later raised to 5,000. Production commenced in March 1944 simultaneously at the Cadillac and Massey-Harris plants, at the same time M5 production ceased. Between April 1944 and August 1945 a total of 4,731 were built. The tank was later named Chaffee, after General Adna A. Chaffee, 'Father' of the US Armored Force.

The tank was first used in action during the Battle of the Bulge and a few (289) were distributed under Lend-Lease for British service. The Chaffee continued in service with the US Army after the war until being replaced by the M41 Walker Bulldog. Although there had been great plans for a family of AFVs known as the 'Light Combat Team' based on the M24, the war ended before this could really get started. The only variants produced were M19GMC - 300 of

Above: **The M5A1 incorporated a larger bulge at the back of the turret to house radio equipment. This one also has a large bin which makes the turret look even longer. Note also the raised rear decking to make room for the twin V-8 Cadillac engines.** *(TM)*

Top: **T77E1 Multiple Gun Motor Carriage was developed in 1943 to mount quadruple .50 HMGs on the M24 chassis. It never went further than prototype stage.** *(TM)*

Above : **Standard production model of the M24 Chaffee light tank, without doubt the best light tank of World WarTwo. The 75mm M6 gun, good armour (up to 25mm) and powerful V-8 Cadillac engines, made it a most valuable asset to any reconnaissance unit.** *(TM)*

these AA tanks (mounting twin 40mm guns) were built and remained standard equipment for many years after the war. It had a crew of six and weighed 17.2tons. M41HMC (Gorilla)- 85 of these fitted with 155mm M1 howitzers were built and also became standard equipment in the post-war US Army. It had a crew of twelve and weighed just under 19tons.

MEDIUM TANKS

Three prototype medium tanks were built in the early 1920s - the Medium A of 1921 and 1922, and the T1 of 1925. They all weighed 20 tons, mounted a 37mm gun and a co-ax MG, plus two MGs in sponsons and two in AA mounts on the turret. Due to the demise of the Tank Corps and the imposition of an upper weight limit of 15tons being placed on medium tanks, none of the three were put into production. Fortunately, however, further development continued and in 1930 the next medium tank appeared. Designated T2, it weighed just under 14tons combat loaded and was powered by a 338hp Liberty engine The armament included a semi-automatic 47mm gun

with a .50 Browning as co-ax MG plus various .30 MGs in sponsons. It had good cross-country performance and externally looked quite similar to the British Vickers Medium Mk II. Three more prototypes were built - T3, T3E2 & T4 all of which were based upon the designs of J Walter Christie. All were fast and reliable, but only lightly armoured. Sixteen T4s were produced at the Rock Island Arsenal - the first time a medium tank had been built in the US in any quantity since World War One.

The next medium tank to appear was the T5, recommended for development in May 1936, it was to be the start of the family which would end with the M4 Sherman, the most widely produced

tank in American history. Armament was to be a 37mm gun and it incorporated many of the features and components on the M2 light tank series (for ease of production) being powered by the same Continental radial engine. Although it began within the 15 ton limit, this did not last, as it was for example re-engined with a larger, more powerful nine-cylinder Wright.

Standardised as the M2 medium tank a contract to build eighteen was issued in the summer of 1939. It now weighed about 20 tons, although the armour plate was still very thin. As the development programme progressed improvements were incorporated, such as making the turret more roomy by having vertical in place

of sloping walls, increasing armoured protection and engine power. The M2A1 was powered by a Wright R975 EC2 air-cooled radial engine, which was similar to the M2's but had power increased to 400hp. The combat weight was now 21 tons. An initial order for 1000 was placed with the Rock Island Arsenal.

Profiting from British battle experience, the Americans now decided that their medium tank needed thicker armour and a more powerful dual purpose gun. After much deliberation it was decided to standardize on the 75mm gun and stayed with this calibre for most of the war until the much improved 76mm came into service. There was not time to produce a new turret for

Above: **An M24 on the advance through Germany, 1945. Entering service in late 1944, it was to be the start of the 'Light Combat Team' however, the war ended before the series could be completed.** *(TM)*

Above: **A column of M3 medium tanks on training in Britain. These are the General Lee version, with the commander's cupola, rivetted hull, side doors and powered by a Wright radial engine. They first entered service in April 1941.** *(TM)*

Right: **A T5 phase III medium tank, photographed at Rock Island Arsenal, 1938. This was the prototype of the standard production M2 medium tank, forerunner of M3 and M4.** *(TM)*

the M2 gun although one was being designed, instead as an interim solution the gun was put into a large sponson on the right hand side of the tank. Ordnance had tried this system out a few months previously and it had worked well, although gun traverse was naturally limited. The new medium tank the M3 was based on the M2A1, it weighed around 28 tons had armour up to 50mm thick, a crew of seven and mounted both a 37mm gun and co-ax MG in a small turret

France, where nearly 700 tanks had been knocked out or abandoned. However, the British commission, demanded certain modifications, including a larger, slightly lower turret with a rear bustle to provide room for the radio (saving one crew member) and removing the very prominent machine-gun cupola.

also a sponson-mounted 75mm. In addition to the US Army, a British tank purchasing commission, which had arrived in June 1940, was also showing considerable interest in the M3 in order to make up for their considerable losses in

From the outset of production, two types of M3 were built - the US Army version known as the General Lee, and the British version the General Grant. Production rate was then around fourteen tanks per day, eight of which were for

Above: **Only twelve M3A2 medium tanks were built between January and March 1942. It featured an all-welded hull but was otherwise identical to the M3.** *(TM)*

Left: **M3A1 had a cast hull but later production models had no side door or floor hatch. A total of 300 were built between February and August 1942.** *(TM)*

Right: **Medium tank M3 serial number 28, the first M3A3, after its trial conversion to diesel power (two GM diesels).** *(TM)*

Right: **The M3A4 was converted from the M3 by fitting a 370hp Chrysler multi-bank engine. The extended hull (20 inches longer) meant there had to be more space between suspension bogies.** *(TM)*

Right: **The M3A5 was the same as the M3A3, but with a rivetted hull and no side doors (on later models). Note also the counterweight on the end of the gun barrel.** *(TM)*

Right: **An American CDL (Canal Defense Light) searchlight tank was designated T10 Shop Tractor for security reasons. The searchlight had a 13,000,000 candle-power beam and shone through a 24 inch vertical slot.** *(TM)*

the US six for Britain. The M3 was of course a stopgap tank and was superseded by the Sherman. However, it did play a significant role in the battles in North Africa. When production ceased in December 1942, many of the 6,000 plus M3s produced were still serviceable and were supplied to many foreign armies around the world.

	M3 – Lee I	M3 – Grant I
Crew	seven	six
Weight	27.45ton	27.68ton
Dimensions		
Length	18ft 6ins	18ft 6ins
Height	10ft 3ins	9ft 11ins
Width	8ft 11ins	8ft 11ins
Armour	12mm-50mm	12mm-50mm
Armament	75mm gun M2 or M3; 37mm gun M5 or M6 and up to four .30 machine guns	
Engine	nine-cylinder Wright (Continental) R975 EC2	
Max speed	21mph	21mph
Radius of action	120miles	120miles

Some six models of the M3 were built between April 1941 and December 1942, the major types being:

M3
Rivetted hull, side doors and Wright radial engine. 4924 built between April 1941-January 1942

M3A1
Cast hull, later production models had no side doors or floor hatch. 300 built between February and August 1942

M3A2
All-welded hull, new engine introduced after two months. Twelve built between January and March 1942

M3A3
As M3A2 but with twin GM diesels, weight now 28.1 tons. 322 built between March and December 1942

M3A4
As for M3 but with 370hp Chrysler multi-bank engine, weight now 28.57ton, 12 inches longer. 109 built between June and August 1942

M3A5
As for M3A3 but with rivetted hull, no side doors on late models. 591 built between January and November 1942

The first M3s to see action were in British army service in the Western Desert, May 1942 in the Gazala line area. American M3s were first used in action just six months later but also in North Africa, after the Operation Torch landings of November 1942.

The M3 chassis was used for a variety of tasks, such as the M33 Prime Mover, an artillery gun tractor, with its armament and turret removed. The M31 tank recovery vehicle, was a standard M3, without main guns (usually with dummy wooden gun barrels in their place), and fitted with a rear-mounted boom and a 60,000lb capacity winch.

The Grant Scorpion III & IV flail-type minefield clearing devices, again without the 75mm gun.

The most interesting variant was the Grant CDL (Canal Defence Light), which, took over from the Matilda CDL. Known also as the T10 Shop Tractor, this secret weapon was meant for D Day, but was not used until the Rhine Crossing.

The M4 Sherman, successor to the M3, began life as the T6 medium tank built in mock-up form in May 1941 and designed to eliminate the four major shortcomings of the M3, namely – limited traverse of main gun, limited performance of main gun, high silhouette, poor armoured protection. However, it was decided to use as many of the tried and tested components of the M3 as possible,

initially the basic chassis, suspension, transmission and engine were all utilised. The major change was the fully traversing turret, mounted in the centre of a new hull, armed with an improved 75mm gun and .30 inch co-ax MG. The crew was five, three in the turret (commander, gunner and loader/radio operator) plus two in the hull (driver and assistant driver/bow gunner). The Americans had accepted the idea of having the radio in the turret, but had (unlike the British) retained the fifth crew member. Changes were made to the mock up, including removing the commander's cupola (to reduce height) and approval was given to build a pilot model with a cast hull, this was completed in September 1941 by the Lima

Above: **The crew of a British manned Sherman stop for a brew at a very muddy location. According to the censor of the time, 'Somewhere in NW Europe'.** *(TM)*

Far right: **Two Sherman M4A3, with welded hulls and one piece cast noses, loaded on a railroad flatcar.** *(TM)*

Right: **Sherman M4(105) mounting a CS 105mm M4 howitzer leads an armoured column through vineyards near the village of Conselics, Italy, April 1944. They are part of the US 8th Army in pursuit of German forces retreating to Modena and Ferrara.** *(GF)*

Right: **A Sherman V (M4A4) being hauled up a steep bank by heavy winches. Note the red-white-red British National Identification Mark, just to the left of the name (ADJUNCT).** *(TM)*

Model	British Name	Main Characteristics	In Service Date	Numbers Built
M4	Sherman 1*a*	Welded hull; Continental R975 engine; early vehicles had a three-piece bolted nose and narrow M34 gun mount; later vehicles had a combination cast and rolled hull front.	July 1942.	674
M4A1	Sherman 2	As for M4 but with cast hull; first model in full production early vehicles had M3-type bogie units, M2, 75mm gun with counterweights, twin fixed MGs in hull front (later eliminated and M3, 75mm gun fitted); nose altered from three-piece bolted to one piece cast; M3A1 mount and sand shields added later.	February 1942.	6281
M4A2	Sherman 3	As for M4 but never had cast/rolled hull; twin GM 6-71 diesel engines fitted.	April 1942.	8053
M4A3	Sherman 4	Welded hull, one piece cast nose; V-8 500hp Ford GAA petrol engine, most advanced of series with 75mm gun; mainly kept for US use.	June 1942	1690
M4A4	Sherman 5	Three-piece bolted nose; 370hp Chrysler WC Multi-bank petrol engine which required lengthening the hull to 19ft 10.5in; increased speed to 25mph.	July 1942.	7499
M4A5		Designation set aside for Canadian Ram II		
M4A6		Final basic model with M4A4 hull and chassis; 450hp Caterpillar RD-1820 diesel radial engine; cast and rolled front.	October 1942.	75
M4(105)		Mounted CS 105mm M4 howitzer in M52 mount in turret.	February 1944.	1641
M4A1(76),			January 1944.	3426
M4A2(76)W *b*			May 1944	2915
M4A3(75)W			February 1944	3071
M4A3(76)W			March 1944	4542
M4A3(105)		Howitzer as for M4(105)	May 1944	3039
M4A3E2		Assault tank (see text)	June 1944.	254
			TOTAL	49,234

Notes: *a. Late production models with cast upper front hull were known as the Sherman Hybrid 1.*

b. 'W' stands for 'Wet Stowage' - ammunition stowed in water-jacketed racks below the turret instead of in the sides (eg: 10 boxes in the hull floor held 100 rounds and needed 37. 1gallons of water, plus a further gallon to protect the four ready rounds. Water contained anti-freeze and Ammudamp a corrosion inhibitor.

Locomotive Works. The main difference between the pilot and T6 was the elimination of the side doors, although the very first one built by Lima used a T6 upper hull casting with the holes welded up. The second had a new hull casting and was sent to Britain. Both pilots were armed with the short 75mm M2 gun, as the new M3 gun was not yet available

It was at this time that President Roosevelt ordered tank production to be doubled, so that 2,000 medium tanks plus 800 lights alone were to be built every month during 1942. This meant finding new plants to produce the new tank, including building from scratch – yet another

Above: **This Sherman M4A1 was very special being the first one the British acquired and the second tank off the production line at the Lima Locomotive Works. It is named MICHAEL after Michael Dewar, who led the British Tank Mission to America.** *(TM)*

Above: **Fording a river in Italy, this Sherman M4A2 (Sherman III) has been fitted with wading trunking over the engine air intake, to keep it clear of water.** *(TM)*

Right: **This M4A3E8 was one of a number of models used to test out the new Horizontal Volute Spring Suspension system(HVSS), which was a significant improvement over the old vertical volute spring (VVS)type.** *(TM)*

massive factory at Grand Blanc, Michigan. Eleven plants in all would build Sherman, producing a staggering 49,234 gun tanks of all types to be used by every Allied nation in just about every theatre of the war and for the widest possible range of armoured tasks.

There were six basic models built between February 1942 and June 1944 as the table shows. The missing M4A5, was allocated by the United States to the Canadian-built Ram II. To these six must also be added seven more gun models (also shown). Later in the war, when the HVSS

Above: **The British called the American M3 light tank the 'Honey' because it was so reliable, easy to drive and maintain. This M3A1 actually came from Brazil where it was in service after World War Two. Still in full running order, it was presented to the Tank Museum, Bovington in April 1990.** *(TM)*

Left: **This immaculate M5A1 is owned by Judge Jim Osborne of the Indiana Military Museum, Vincennes, USA. The M5A1 was the last of the M3 M5 line and was powered by twin V-8 Cadillac petrol engines.**
(J. Osborne)

Above: **M3 General Grant in desert camouflage. Note the canvas dust cover over the sponson-mounted gun's mantlet.** *(TM)*

Above and left: **The Americans named their M3 as the General Lee whilst the British version was known as the General Grant. The Grant had a specially built turret (without the extra four inches high commander's cupola) incorporating a large bustle for radio equipment. Both weighed around 27.5 tons and were armed with a sponson-mounted 75mm gun, a 37mm in the turret and up to four machine guns, including one co-axially mounted with the 37mm. Over 6,000 M3s were produced.** *(TM)*

Above: **The M 4 Sherman medium tank was probably the Western Allies' most significant tank of World War Two. Nearly 50,000 were built and served with all Allied armies in every theatre of the war. Reliable and with an excellent cross-country performance, it as well-liked by crews.** *(TM)*

Right: **The Canadians built the Ram medium tank at the same time as the Americans were producing the M3. They then designed the 'Sherman Grizzly', 200 of which were built, based on the cast-hull Sherman M4A1.** *(TM)*

Above: **Only two pilot models of the 47-ton Assault Tank T 14 were ever built. In August 1943, one was sent to Britain and the other being tested in the United States. The project was cancelled four months later, but the T14 sent to Britain has been preserved at the Tank Museum.** *(TM)*

Left: **A Sherman A4A1E8 (76) restored to full running order at the Indiana Military Museum, Vincennes, USA. The 76mm replaced the 75mm gun, giving the Sherman more firepower.** *(J. Osborne)*

Right: **Sherman was used for a wide variety of special purpose vehicles, the most successful being the Sherman Crab minefield gapping device. Here the flail jib is in the raised, travelling position.** *(IM)*

Below: **The rotary chain flail (43 chains), powered from the main tank engine, beat the ground ahead of the tank detonating mines.** *(TM)*

Above: **Sherman M32 Tank Recovery Vehicle, was equipped with a jib and a powerful 60,000lb winch. It also mounted an 81mm mortar, so that a smoke screen could be created as cover for operations (not fitted on this vehicle).** *(TM)*

Left: **The Ram Kangaroo APC (Armoured Personnel Carrier) could carry eleven fully equipped soldiers as well as a crew of two.** *(TM)*

Above and right: **The M24 Chaffee, mounted a powerful 76mm gun, with firepower equal to that of many medium tanks. Chaffees first saw action during the Battle of the Bulge in the Ardennes, Belgium. Nearly 5,000 were built and the M24 continued in service after World War Two. It was also used in action during the Korean War.** *(TM)*

Left: **On exercises before D-Day, 1944, this Sherman M4A6 is passing through a town in England. All identification (shop and street names) has been obliterated by the censor's red pen.** *(TM)*

Below: **The 37.5 ton T14 assault tank was built in 1943 to fill a requirement from both the American and British armies for a heavy assault tank.** *(TM)*

Bottom: **The Sherman M4 (105) the close support version which mounted a 105mm howitzer. Known by the British as the Sherman B.** *(TM)*

suspension and 27-inch tracks were introduced the suffix 'Y' was added. The British also used the following nomenclature to differentiate between gun types:

Sherman	- 75mm
Sherman A	- 76mm
Sherman B	- 105mm
Sherman C	- 17 pounder

The Sherman's basic characteristics varied quite considerably with model, armament, etc, as can be seen from a comparison of the specifications of an early M4 with a late M4A2(76)W.

Specification	M4	M4A2(76)W
Battle weight	29.87 tons	32.77 tons
Dimensions		
Length	19ft 4ins	24ft 10ins
Width	8ft 7ins	8ft 9ins
Height	9ft	9ft 9ins
Armour	13–88mm	13–106mm
Armament	75mm gun M3	76mm gun M1A1
	plus .5 MG, two .30 MG (one co-ax) and one 2 inch mortar M3 (smoke) fixed in turret	
Engine	nine-cylinder Wright R975C1 radial	Twin GM 6046 twelve-cylinder inline diesel
Max speed	24 mph	30 mph
Range	120 miles	100 miles

Right: **An infantry
squad follows a
Sherman M4A1
during training in
Britain prior to
D-Day. Although
all the crew
hatches are open,
the commander is
still sensibly
keeping his head
down. Many tank
commanders were
killed by enemy
snipers.** (TM)

Improvements were made as tank building
progressed, the most important being the up
gunning to 76mm which had an increased muzzle
velocity and better performance:

Soon after D-Day, 138 of the newly armed
Shermans were sent to Normandy but it was soon
found that the new gun would not penetrate the
front armour plate of either Panther or Tiger (both

Below: **Shermans of
the Chinese-
American 1st
Provisional Tank
Group, which
operated in Burma,
early 1945.** (TM)

Type of gun		Muzzle Velocity	Weight of Projectile	500	1000	1500	2000
					Penetration in mm at		
75mm	APCBC	1930	14.4		62	48	40
	APC	2030	14.96	70	59	55	50
76.2mm	APCBC	2600	15.44	94	89	81	76

100mm thick). A new ammunition-high velocity armour piercing (HVAP) M9 shot was being developed, which was eventually effective. However, in the meantime the only Sherman which could deal effectively with enemy heavy tanks was the British version which mounted a high velocity 17 pounder gun. Known as the Sherman Firefly, there were three models: the Sherman IIC - designation for the M4A1 with 17 pounder; the Sherman IVC - an M4A3 with 17 pounder; and Sherman VC - an M4A4 with 17 pounder. British Sherman units had one Firefly in each troop. The US Army tried to acquire the 17 pounder for their Shermans, but British ordnance factories were working to capacity and unable to supply. As General Omar Bradley rightly commented: 'Our tank superiority devolved primarily from a superiority in the number rather than the quality of tanks we sent into battle'.

Up-armouring was tried, the most extreme example being the Jumbo Sherman which weighed over 6 tons heavier than the normal M4. It was developed in early 1944 as an assault tank when it became clear that the new heavy tank, T26E1, would not enter service until 1945. The project had begun life in July 1943, when two pilot models of the 47-ton T14 assault tank were built. One was sent to Britain (and is still on show at Bovington) the other to Fort Knox, however, the project was cancelled. Nevertheless, there remained the need for a heavily armoured tank (the British alone had said they required some

Below: **Crossing a shallow river in Italy, next to a Roman aqueduct is this Chrysler multi-bank engined Sherman M4A4. The triangle is the tactical sign for A Squadron.** *(TM)*

Right: **Heaviest of all Shermans was 'Jumbo', an M4A3 which had extra armour added up to a maximum thickness of 100mm on the hull. The turret had 150mm of frontal armour. Its weight was increased to 42 tons. Known as the M4A3E2, over 250 were built by Grand Blanc between May and June 1944. These were rushed to Europe where they performed very well. A few were refitted with 76mm guns but most had the standard 75mm.** *(TM)*

Below: **Mine Excavator T5E2. Developed in late 1943, this was a type of mine plough which had the arms and hydraulic lift gear from the M1 dozer fitted.** *(TM)*

8,500 assault tanks), so additional armour was added to the M4A3 Sherman to give the hull a maximum thickness of 102mm. A new cast turret with armour 153mm thick was designed, all of which increased the weight to 42 tons and reduced the speed to 22 mph. Permanent Grousers (known as 'duckbills') were added to the tracks allowing better cross-country performance. Between May and June 1944 a total of 254 were built. Designated Sherman M4A3E2, these were shipped to Europe in autumn 1944 and proved very effective.

As the table shows five different engines were used in the Sherman, but this was done more for ease of production than to increase the mobility. One minor invention which certainly did assist in mobility by dealing with the confining hedgerows of the Normandy bocage country, was the Culin Hedgerow Cutter. Named after its inventor

Above: **Mine Resistant Vehicle T15E1 of 1944. This extraordinary looking vehicle was a heavily armoured Sherman body fitted with heavy duty tracks and suspension. It was designed to be driven over the mines and explode them. The project was abandoned when war ended.** *(TM)*

Left: **Mine Exploder T3E2. A development of the T3 which itself followed the British use of a rotor drum and flails (Matilda Scorpion), it had a large diameter drum instead of the rotor. Project abandoned when the war ended.** *(TM)*

Sergeant G. Culin, of 102nd Cavalry Reconnaissance Squadron, it was more usually known as Rhinoceros, it comprised a tusk-like structure of welded angle iron mounted on the front of the tank and used to cut into the base of the hedge. The tank could then burst through the hedge without having to climb over and needlessly expose its underside.

As with the M3, the British Army used the M4 in action before the US Army. North Africa was again the battlefield and the famous battle of El Alamein, October 1942. The Americans used theirs in Tunisia, in January 1942. Later they were used all over the world, building up a reputation for reliability and good cross-country performance but unfortunately also for catching fire easily – the GIs called it the Ronson Lighter ('guaranteed to light first time') and the Germans, the 'Tommy Cooker'.

Of all the tanks used in World War Two the Sherman was undoubtedly the most adaptable and its chassis was fitted with a wide variety of specialized equipment, by both the Americans and British. These included armoured recovery vehicles, earth moving equipment, mine clearing equipment, gap crossing equipment, amphibious equipment, engineer equipment, flamethrowers, rocket launchers, SP artillery, armoured personnel carriers, cargo carriers and prime movers.

One of the greatest concentrations of the above types equipped the British 79th Armoured Division commanded by Major General P C S Hobart, and known affectionately as the Funnies. This was a very special armoured formation, larger than any other in 21st Army Group and

Right: **Beach Armoured Recovery Vehicle (BARV). This was a British adaptation of the Sherman ARV Mk I, for use on beach landings. Over 50 were delivered by D-Day and proved to be most useful rescuing swamped vehicles.** *(TM)*

Left: **The most successful type of minefield gapping equipment was the British Sherman Crab also operated by US troops. It had forty-three flailing chains on a rotor which beat the ground just ahead of the tank, exploding mines,** *(TM)*

Left: **A Sherman T9 mine exploder towing its heavy roller - in action of course it would have been pushed in front to explode the mines.** *(TM)*

Above: **The British-invented Bullshorn Plough had one ploughshare fitted ahead of each track. They were used by the 79th Armoured Division on the Normandy beaches, 1944. The photograph is of the equipment on trials in a snow storm.** *(TM)*

was formed for the D-Day landings, its specialized armour making a major contribution to the success of the landings.

Recovery Vehicles - US Army tank recovery vehicles were known under the M32 designation, and carried an A-frame boom approximately 18feet long and a powered winch. Armament comprised: an 81mm mortar on the front plate, a .50 HMG on the fixed turret and a .30 MG in the bow. Types were:- M32 - based on M4; M32B1 - based on M4A1; M32B2 - based on M4A2; M32B3 - based on M4A3 and the M32B4 - based on M4A4. In addition there was another series, based upon the M4 with HVSS and 23 inch tracks; the M32A1

based on M4 and M32A1B1 based on M4A1.

British types were Sherman III, ARV MkI and Sherman V, ARV Mk I - both turretless. Sherman V, ARV Mk II - fabricated turret with dummy gun, winch and lifting gear. Sherman IIA (M32) ARV Mk III - standard M32. Sherman BARV - with armoured superstructure and deep wading gear for seaborne assault.

Earth Movers - a few M4s were fitted with dozer blades and hydraulic hoists taken from Caterpillar D-8 bulldozers in Italy. They were so successful that a special M1 blade was designed and produced for the M4. A second, wider version M1A1 was also made to work with tanks fitted with

HVSS and 23inch tracks. A few M4 dozers, permanently allocated to the engineers had their turrets removed.

Mine Clearing Devices - a fairly large number of devices were tried out with the Sherman as the prime mover, these were mainly rollers, flails and ploughs. The roller detonated by pressure, the flail by beating the ground in which the mine was buried and thus exploding it, while the plough exposed mines for the engineers to make safe. A few rollers (T1E3(M1) Aunt Jemima built in 1943) saw limited battle service, however, the most successful were undoubtedly the flails , like the British-designed Scorpion and Crab.

US types - Rollers. Mine Exploder - T1E1 Earthworm - three sets of six large discs in a tri-cycle pattern. T1E2 - modified T1E1 with two sets of seven discs. T1E3 (M1) Aunt Jemima - two sets of

Above: **A well restored example of a late production M32B1, Sherman Tank Recovery Vehicle.** *(TM)*

Left: **The Mine Exploder T8, also known as 'Johnnie Walker' a six steel plunger exploder unit on a pivoted frame. It proved impossible to steer and was abandoned.** *(TM)*

five discs. T1E4 - sixteen large discs in a single curved boom. T1E5 - two units of six discs attached to a centre frame. T1E6 - as for T1E3, but with serrated- edged discs. T7 - frame of small rollers, each of two discs. T9 - heavy studded six foot roller attached to a frame. T9E1 - six foot cast steel roller, 10 feet wide attached to a long rotating tube. T10 - modified M4 mounted above an articulated tricycle unit of three rollers.

Flails - T2, T3, T3E1, T3E2 & T4 were all flails similar to British models.

Ploughs - Mine Excavator T2E2, T4, T5, T5E3 & T6 were all plough devices with various types of blades.

Miscellaneous - T8 - vibrating steel plungers on a pivoted frame . T11 - six spigot mortars. T12 - spigot mortar launching platform with 23 tubes on a turretless M4. T14, T15, T15E1 T15E2 - mine resistant tanks with extra armour.

British types - These were mainly flails and explosive devices, the latter being hoses full of explosives which blew a lane through a minefield. Also used was the Canadian Indestructible Roller Device (CIRD).

Flails - Pram Scorpion - a combination of flails and rollers. Marquis - flail like Crab II, but the tank had a large welded, flat-sided turret (for hydraulic rams and drive motor). Sherman Crab I -

Above: **These engineers have the unenviable task of getting a track back on their Sherman M1 Dozer.** *(TM)*

Right: **Invented by Nicholas Straussler the Duplex Drive (DD) for amphibious tanks, incorporated a collapsible canvas screen to turn the tank into a boat. Two small swivelling propellers allowed steerage, whilst the tracks rotating assisted forward propulsion. Used very successfully by the British on D-Day.** *(TM)*

rotary chain flail, working off the engine, with 43 chains. Sherman Crab II – similar but with a contouring device, making it more effective on ridges and furrows. Bullshorn Plough – as used by 79th Armoured Division.

Explosive devices – Sherman with 3 inch Snake – explosive packed into water piping – blew 21 feet long gap. Sherman with Conger – 330 yards of 2 inch woven hose (carried in a towed engineless Bren carrier fitted with a rocket projector) fired across the minefield, the hose pumped full of explosive, then detonated. Sherman with CIRD and Tapeworm – a trailer containing 50 yards of $2\frac{3}{4}$ inch canvas hose, packed with explosive and towed behind tank fitted with CIRD. Sherman with CIRD and Bangalore Flying torpedos each dual projector was fitted either side of the roller, the four torpedoes were fitted with small grapnels

Miscellaneous – Sherman CIRD – two types of rollers ($15\frac{1}{2}$ and 18 inch) were used, being able to 'jump' when mines were detonated.

Bridges – M4 mobile assault bridge – field

tank to pass through a flame barrage. DD II Ginandit – a matting device to enable DD to negotiate mud flats.

Flame – A wide variety of flameguns were fitted, either in place of hull MG or in the turret with or in place of main armament. These included using the Canadian Ronson flamegun and the British Churchill Crocodile flame equipment. US nomenclatures included E4R2-5R1, E4R3-5R1 (M3-4-3); E4R4-4R 5-6RC; POA, POA-CWS 75-H1, POA-CWS 75-H2; E6-R1 and E7-7. British designations were Adder, Salamander, Crocodile and Badger.

Rockets – These were fitted, mainly in tubes over the turret. A few saw operational service, such as: T34 (Calliope) – sixty 4.6inch rocket tubes in

Below: **T31 Demolition tank was an experimental model which had a 105mm howitzer mounted in a strangely-shaped large turret, with a 7.2inch rocket projector on each side.** *(TM)*

modification in Italy using a double-track bridge supported on an A-frame jib when travelling. The bridge could not be recovered once dropped, the tank also required heavy ballast at the rear. Sherman Twaby Ark – M4 fitted with British Churchill Ark equipment (Octopus was a variant). Sherman Plymouth – turret removed and length of Bailey bridge in its place.

Amphibious – M19 Swimming device – metal buoyancy tanks filled with plastic foam fitted around tank, detached by explosive charges on landing. Used in the Pacific. British Sherman Duplex Drive (DD), Straussler equipment converted a standard tank into a temporary amphibian, using a collapsible canvas screen fitted with rubber tubes (for erection by compressed air – this took approximately 15 minutes) and a metal frame for support. Two small propellers at the rear were driven off the tank's bevel-drive and gave a speed in the water of 4mph (steered by swivelling the propellers). Its crews were equipped with Davis underwater escape apparatus. DD with Belch – piping fitted around the top of the DD screen from which jets of sea water were sprayed allowing the

Left: **A British-adapted Sherman CDL 'E' unit, with a combination welded/cast turret, the only armament being a single ball-mounted machine gun. Note the slits for two lights.** *(TM)*

four sets of fifteen on a frame above the turret. T40(M17) (Whizz-Bang) - twenty 7.2inch rockets in a jettisonable box-like frame, fired by the main gun control. A British (Guards Armoured Division) modification had a 60lb aircraft-type rocket fitted on a launch rail at the side of the turret.

Gun Mounts - Demolition tank T31 - 105mm howitzer, with 7.2inch rocket projectors on each side of a heavily armoured turret. Multiple GMC T52 - either two 40mm AA, or a 40mm plus two .50 HMG, and the GMC T53 - 90mm gun.

Miscellaneous - Sherman Kangaroo - the British stripped out around 75 Sherman IIIs in Italy 1944 to use as APCs (as RAM). Sherman fascine carrier (carried up to three fascines) - This was a British conversion of older type Shermans. Sherman gun tractor, to tow 17pounder anti-tank guns in Italy. M34 full-track prime mover - modification of M32B1 recovery vehicle to tow heavy artillery, the A-frame and winch being removed.

HEAVY TANKS

Even when equipped with the 76mm gun, the Sherman did not have sufficient firepower nor was its armoured protection good enough to allow it to survive on the battlefield. Its mobility was undisputed as was its general maneuverability, although both were capable of being improved by fitting a more powerful engine and better suspension. Almost as soon as the M4 design was completed, work had begun on its successor this being designated the M4X. The basic specification was for a five-man tank with the same general layout as Sherman, but much more streamlined, with armour up to 100mm (front) a lower silhouette, armed with the new 76mm M1 gun and powered by a V-8 Ford GAN engine. In May 1942, a mock-up was built by the Product Study Design Team of General Motors, this was enthusiastically received, the tank being designated T20 and authority given to build two pilots then a further four – two designated T22 and two T23. Of the six tanks, T20, T22 & T23 three were to be equipped with the 76mm M1 gun, while the other three, T20E1, T22E1 & T23E1 would have the 75mm M3 gun with an autoloader in a special turret.

The preliminary tests on the T23 pilot models proved to be so promising that a contract to produce 250 tanks was issued in May 1943. Fifty of these would be modified to fit the newly developed 90mm gun, forty of which would have the same armour as the T23 but the other ten would have thicker armour. The two models were designated as T25 and T26 and after much trials work, the T26 was chosen. The T26E1 followed, which had hydramatic transmission with a torque converter,

Left: **Calliope, T34 rocket launcher had sixty 90 inch long plastic tubes into which 4.6 in rockets were loaded. Developed in 1943, it was used in combat in 1944 and proved to be very effective. The mount was harmonized with the traverse and elevating mechanism of the gun barrel.** *(TM)*

Above: **A Sherman M4A1 (76mm gun) mounting an M3-4-3 flamegun in place of the hull machine gun. It had a range of approximately 60 yards.** *(TM)*

Right: **A Sherman Crab MK II of 30 Armoured Brigade, 79th Armoured Division, on a Normandy beach. Of the 30 deployed twelve were destroyed. Note the engine wading breather at the rear.** *(GF)*

in place of the heavier more complicated electric transmission in the T26. In comparison trials at Fort Knox, it was found that although the T26 model had a better overall performance on normal terrain the electric transmission was considered far too complicated for battlefield repair, so the T26E1 was chosen.

Early in June 1944, those at the 'sharp end' in the European Theatre of Operations (ETO) stated that they did not want any new tanks with 75mm or 76mm guns, instead they needed tanks with 90mm and 105mm guns (in the ratio four to one). This request was approved by the Army Staff and the T26E1 trials continued, and by the end of that month the tank was reclassified as the heavy tank T26E1.

It should have been plain sailing from then onwards, especially as it was recommended 1,500 should be built immediately. However, for some

unaccountable reason the Armored Force said they only wanted 500, while Army Ground Forces said the tank should be redesigned to mount the 76mm gun! This in fighting led to more delays, so it was not until December 1944 that a limited procurement order was finally approved. The first twenty T26E3s were finally shipped out to the ETO in January 1945 and first saw action in February. Their excellent battlefield performance quickly convinced the Army Ground Forces, who then immediately requested as many of the new tanks as possible to be sent as fast as possible! Full production began and in March 1945, the tank was formally standardised as the heavy tank M26. It was named Pershing, after General 'Black Jack' Pershing of Mexican War and World War One fame. Total wartime production was 1,436 but a further 992 were built in late 1945. Of all these only 310 ever reached the ETO and 200 were

Above: **The British Sherman Firefly was undoubtedly the best armed of all Shermans, its 17 pounder gun matching the firepower of Tiger - but not the same level of protection. Usually one Firefly was deployed in each tank troop.** *(GF)*

Right: **The Heavy Tank M6A1, weighed 56.48 tons was armed with a 3 inch gun also a 37mm and four MGs. It was never used in action and in December 1944 the series was declared obsolete.** *(TM)*

Right: **The T25 pilot Number 1 was tested at APG in late January 1944. It had HVSS suspension and a 90mm gun mounted in a large turret. It was dropped in favour of the T26.** *(TM)*

issued to units. Of these only twenty ever saw any kind of action. Some were also dispatched to Okinawa, arriving in July 1945, but were never used before VJ-Day. The Pershing would have to wait until the Korean War to show its true worth.

M26 Pershing	
Crew	five (three in turret, two in hull)
Weight (tons)	41.23
Dimensions	
Length	28ft 4½ins
Width	11ft 6ins
Height	9ft 1in
Armament	90mm M3 gun, two .30 MG (one co-ax, one bow) and one .50 AA
Armour	12.5mm to 112.5mm (on gunshield)
Engine	V-8 500hp Ford GAN petrol
Max speed	30 mph
Range	100 miles

Just like other tank building nations, the United States dabbled with the idea of building a super heavy tank. In May 1940, it was initially envisaged as an 80 ton tank, with two turrets each housing a 75mm gun (partial traverse) and two more turrets with 37mm

Below: **The 'Super Pershing' as fitted up in the field by 2nd Armoured Division. The two cylinders above the gun contain coil springs as weight compensators for the new 90mm T15E1 gun. More armour plate (from a Panther) has been welded to the gunshield and added to the front glacis plate.** *(GF)*

Left: **'Tiger Tamer'. The T26E3 General Pershing was the most powerful US tank to see operational service. However, it was only ever used in small numbers before the war finished.** *(TM)*

guns and machine guns. Armour was to be at least 75mm thick. By October 1940, they had revised the specification for the heavy tank T1 which would now weigh about 50 tons; mount a 3-inch gun and coaxial 37 mm in a single turret, four machine guns; armour still at 75mm; powered by a 925hp Wright engine with hydramatic transmission, and able to achieve a top speed of 25mph. In February 1941 it was agreed to build four pilots each with different hulls, transmissions (including electric) and other components. The first pilot completed was the T1E2 in December 1942, just after the attack on Pearl Harbour. It was 27ft 8ins long, 10ft 7ins high and 10ft 2½ins wide with armour 25 to 100mm thick. After some modification it was standardised as the M6. Next completed was the T1E3, standardised as the

Above: **This interesting line-up compares an M6 heavy tank with the M3 light tank and M3 medium tank. Despite its size and gun power the M6 did not impress the Armored Force.** *(TM)*

Right: **One of the newly-arrived Pershings being unloaded using a 100-ton crane, Antwerp docks, Belgium, January 1945. Of the 200 issued to units only 20 saw any action.** *(TM)*

Below: **The Pershing, was fitted with a well-shaped, spacious turret mounting a 90mm gun.** *(TM)*

M6A1 and differed only by having a welded hull. The original production requirement of 100 vehicles a month was raised to 250, with a total procurement of 5,000 envisaged. However, under a rationalisation programme between the Services, this was cut drastically to a mere 115 in favour of aircraft production.

Meanwhile the Armored Force had been testing the pilot models and did not like the new tank finding it too heavy, under-gunned and not the right shape, so therefore only of limited use. In March 1943, production was slashed again to just forty vehicles, all being built between November 1942 and February 1944. Although

this 56.5 ton monster was originally when planned, one of the heaviest, largest and most powerfully armed tanks in the world none saw operational service. Instead they proved useful as trials vehicles, being used for testing the T1E1 electric transmission later used in the T23 and also the 90mm gun for T26E1. The nearest it came to being used in action was in July 1944, when the ETO made an urgent request for heavy tanks, so one M6A2 was modified with a new heavy turret mounting a 105mm gun. It was planned to convert fifteen M6A2s and ship them to Europe, but the project was cancelled and in December 1944 the tank was declared obsolete.

CHAPTER FIVE

Soviet Union

Study and master this machine! Become familiar with the
rudiments of this trampling steel colossus; this demon of fury,
backed by the power of your proletarian strength, will spread terror
amongst the ranks of our enemies.

Youth Commissar Skonyevsko, 1934

The Red Army did not really begin to take
much interest in tank development until
1929, at the beginning of their first Five
Year Plan. Before then, they had dabbled
in armoured warfare, with a mixture of foreign
bought AFVs, whilst the main Soviet tank had
been a copy of the ubiquitous Renault FT 17
(known as the Russkey Renault). Joseph Stalin
supposedly took a great interest in tank design
and production, which naturally helped in
establishing a large and flourishing tank building
industry. Certainly the Supreme Soviet of the
1920s and 1930s gave their approval to the
devoting of a large amount of the nation's
resources to tank building, being determined to
surpass the tank forces of all the other nations. In
the Red Army, People's Commissar for Military
Affairs, Kliment Yefremovich Voroshilov – who
would eventually reach the rank of Marshal, have
a tank named after him (the KV heavy tank), but
then fall out of favour – was a prime instigator of
this work. He also realised that, although
inevitably, the Communist Soviet Union would
have to fight Fascist Germany, it was initially
sensible to co-operate with them on tank design,
building and testing, so that they the Soviets,
could gain useful knowledge. This led to a
combined Russo-German project, the
establishment of a secret tank development school
at Kazan on the Volga.

During the first Five Year Plan, commencing
in 1929, many new, but relatively unsuccessful

tanks were produced, whilst the Germans
brought the prototypes of their new tanks to
Kazan for secret testing. The Soviets also
purchased various types of tank from abroad for
evaluation and to copy. The first Red Army
mechanised brigade (two tank and two motor
rifle battalions, plus reconnaissance and artillery
battalions and supporting services) was formed in
May 1930 and from then on numbers of
armoured formations increased.

The second Five Year Plan was much more
successful than the first from the Red Army's
point of view, the military budget being
quadrupled to five thousand million roubles,
allowing the output of motor vehicles and tanks
to be enormously increased. By the mid-1930s,
according to a German estimate, the Soviets had
some 10,000 tanks far more than anyone else in
the world. Soviet tactical thinking at that time
favoured tank heavy organisations, with the
deep penetration theories of Marshal Mikhail
Tukhachevsky and Colonel Kalinovsky in favour
and enshrined in Red Army field regulations of
1936. These theories owed much to the
teachings of foreigners like Liddell Hart but
found little favour with Stalin, who considered
them to be 'reactionary, decadent and
capitalistic'. In any case, Stalin was about to
purge the Red Army and would kill many of his
most able soldiers. In 1937, Tuchachevsky was
shot by firing squad, his writings destroyed and
his teachings eradicated from the Red Army. In

their place the Soviets embraced the ideas of General Dmitry Pavlov, a so-called tank expert, who had been in Spain where he had seen Russian T-26 light tanks falling easy prey to enemy anti-tank guns. He reported to Stalin and Voroshilov, that: 'the tank can play no independent role on the battlefield', so the Red Army dismantled its independent armour heavy formations and spread their massive tank force in small units throughout its infantry formations, in much the same way as the French - and with similar results, as would be seen in the German success during Barbarossa.

Over the period 1935 to 1938, the Red Army doubled its offensive capability, including (according to reports in Pravda), increasing tank numbers to well over 10,000. They included both amphibians and well-armed heavy tanks, although the majority were light tanks and tankettes. The Soviets had far too many different models in service at the start of the Great Patriotic War - as they called World War Two, including quite a number of obsolete or obsolescent models, many of which were still in front line service.

The chosen policy of standardization using just three types; light, medium and heavy tanks had not yet taken effect. For example, of the 2,794 tanks built in the Soviet Union during 1940, only 115 were T-34s - the Red Army's most modern and powerful medium tank. Repair and recovery was also difficult as many

of the older types were notoriously difficult to maintain. Although on the eve of Barbarossa in June 1941, the Red Army had over 4.5 million men under arms, over 20,000 tanks and 14,000 aircraft, much of this 'strength' would be just so much cannon fodder to the Panzerwaffe. Soviet tank losses, firstly in the Russo-Finnish Winter War (November 1939 to March 1940) and then during the first six months of the German invasion, June 1941 were staggering – the estimate being in excess of 1,600 against the Finns, then ten times that figure, 16-17,000 against the Germans.

Soviet Tank & SP Gun Production		
Year	Numbers	to add to the estimated
1939	2,950	10,000 tanks already in
1940	2,794	service before 1939
1941	6,590	plus some 22,800 AFVs
1942	24,446	supplied via Lend-Lease
1943	24,089	by USA, GB and Canada
1944	28,963	
1945	15,419	
TOTAL	105,251	

Author's note: The total above includes self-propelled gun production, and it is difficult to separate out pure tank numbers, although Zaloga and Grandsen, in their book *Soviet Tanks and Combat Vehicles of WW2*, state that total Soviet wartime tank production was 79,611, some 25,640 less than that given above,

Right: **The T-27A was the licence-built version of the Carden-Loyd tankette, but with full-width overhead protection for the crew. A total of 4,000 T-27s were built.** *(TM)*

but also say that the total production of AFVs was 102,000. Clearly it depends upon what one counts as a tank and what as an SP gun, but I would be inclined to favour the lower figure if tanks ONLY are to be counted. However, what is clear is that the Soviet Union was able to out produce Germany to an astonishing degree, despite all its problems. Nevertheless, what must also be borne in mind is the disproportionate rate of tank losses in favour of the Panzerwaffe - as high as nearly 8 to 1 in 1942, which did not start to reduce until 1943 when the Red Army's skill and expertise began to improve, rough parity being reached by the

Below: **T-26S was the final production model of the T-26 light tank series. It mounted a 45mm gun and weighed 10.3 tons.** *(TM)*

end of 1944. Attrition was so severe at the start of the Great Patriotic War, that it took Soviet industry most of the war years to recover to their 1941, pre-invasion numbers.

LIGHT TANKS

The Soviets entered the Great Patriotic War with a mass of light tanks, and most of their tank building industry geared to their production. However, like the other major protagonists of World War Two, the Soviet Union quickly found, through the hard lessons of battle experience, that the light tank did not have sufficient firepower or protection to survive for long on the modern battlefield. Although the building of light tanks initially increased in the first half of the war, by 1943 production had dropped considerably and later, ceased altogether as they were unable to design the ideal light tank.

The T-27 tankette, which was a licence-built version of the British Carden-Loyd Mk VI tankette, had a wider, longer crew compartment with overhead cover, but the armour was still very thin (4-9mm). The two-man, 1.7ton tankette was powered by a GAZ truck engine and had a top speed of around 22mph. Ideal for training, there was at one time a plan to fit a 37mm gun, but this was dropped. In 1932 around 5,000 were supposed to be built, but actual production was only about one-third of that figure. Most of these had been relegated to training units by the late 1930s, or used for towing anti-tank guns, or as SP mountings for artillery and rocket launchers. Some were still in service at the start of the Great Patriotic War.

Another British design, built under licence in

Left: **The OT-130 was the first flamethrower version of the T-26B-1 and saw service in the early years of World War Two.** *(TM)*

the early 1930s, was the Vickers 6 ton, designated T-26, the series being as follows:

T-26A-1: the original Vickers Model A (twin turret) also known as the TMM1.

T-26A-2. Russian-built with two 7.62mm MG.

T-26A-3: same but 12.7mm gun in righthand turret.

T-26A-4: same but 27mm gun in righthand turret.

T-26A-5: same but 37mm long-barrelled gun in righthand turret.

T-26V-1: commander's version, righthand turret mounted 20mm MG, frame aerial around turret.

T-26V: main commander's version from T-26A-4 or T-26A-5: again with frame aerial around turret.

OT-26: the flamethrower version of the T-26A, with the lefthand turret removed and a flamegun fitted in righthand turret (O: *Ogniemietny* - flamethrower).

From 1933 onwards, production of the twin turret version ceased and instead a single turret version, based on the Vickers Model B (also known as the TMM2) was built. Destined for use by the mechanised cavalry, this had a new larger turret originally designed for BT tanks. The series was:

T-26B-1: round turret with 37mm gun (later models a 45mm).

T-26B-2: improved model from 1937, cast turret with 45mm plus co-ax MG.

AT-1: was an experimental glider version of T-26B-1, with wings and twin-boom tail.

OT-130: flamethrower version (two models) of T-26B-1 or B-2.

T-26B-1(V) & 2(V): commander's tank, fitted with radio and frame aerial around turret.

AT-26: artillery tank version of T-26B-1, mounting a 76.2mm gun and one MG, only a few ever built.

All models in the T-26 series weighed in the region of 8.5tons, had a crew of three, and armour 6-15mm thick. Top speed was 22mph.

The T-26 went into action in Spain during the Civil War (1936-39), whilst some were used by the Red Army against the Japanese in Manchuria, 1939 and at the same time in the Russo-Finnish War of 1939-40.

Disappointing reports from the first two of these wars prompted a redesign of the T-26, with thicker, better sloped armour, lower silhouette and a new semi-conical turret. It was known as the T-26-S (also sometimes as the T-26-C) and had thicker armour (6-25mm), was of welded construction throughout, weighed 10.3tons and mounted a 45mm gun plus two machine guns.

Some of the existing T-26B-2s were modernised, by fitting the new turret, but without the rear machine gun. One other new feature was that all T-26S were fitted with radio, with a rod aerial replacing the frame-type. There was also a flamethrower version known as OT-133 which appeared during the Winter War in Finland.

In total 4,500 of the T-26 series were built before production ended in 1939. Many were lost in 1941-42 and surviving tanks were converted as gun tractors and put to other uses, the most bizarre being to remove their turrets, and fill the chassis full of explosives to be used as radio-controlled mobile mines!

The T-46 was an improved version of the T-26 with the Christie-type suspension from the BT fast tank series. Only seventy were built before it was found to be too complex and expensive to mass produce. The T-46 was used in action against Finland, 1940.

The T-40 was built as the replacement for the T-27, T-30, T-37, T-37A and T-38 light

amphibious tank. It had built-in hull flotation tanks and two versions were produced; T-40 and T-40A improved, distinguished by a more

streamlined nose. The T-40S was the improved production model with thicker armour, but minus propellers making it heavier and of course no

Left: **The T-70, was built to improve the armour and firepower of the light tank series and featured a new welded turret also thicker hull armour.** *(TM)*

longer amphibious. It weighed close to 6.2tons, had a crew of two and mounted a 12.7mm MG or 20mm gun plus an MG.

The T-50 was built to replace the T-26, and was fitted with torsion-bar suspension, a cast turret (with commander's cupola), was more streamlined and had thicker armour. However, being extremely difficult to mass produce, only sixty-five were ever built. The T-60 was a completely new model, based upon the T-40 but not amphibious. It was armed with a Swedish Landswerk 20mm aircraft cannon and from early 1942 was followed by the T-60A, which had solid disc road wheels instead of the spoked type. Over 6000 were built by 1943 when production ended.

Specifications	T-50	T-60	T-70/T-80
Weight (tons)	13.5	5.75	9.05
Crew	four	two	two
Dimensions			
Length:	17ft	13ft 1in	15ft 3ins
Width:	8ft 1in	7ft 6ins	7ft 7ins
Height:	6ft 7ins	6ft 7ins	7ft 6ins
Armour thickness	12-37mm	7-25mm	10-60mm
Armament	45mm	20mm	45mm
	two MG	one MG	one MG
Engine	30hp	85hp	two 70hp
	diesel	petrol	petrol
Top speed	32.5mph	27mph	32mph

Note: T-80 had extra armour but was otherwise very similar to T-70.

This was followed by T-70 and T-70A, built in order to improve on the armour and firepower limitations of the T-60. Over 8,200 were produced by 1944. The final model, T-80, appeared towards the end of 1943 and was based on the T-70, but with welded-on extra

hull armour and fitted with a new wider, more heavily armoured turret.

The T-70 chassis was used to mount one or two SU-37 AA guns, while T-60s were used to mount the *Katyushka* rocket launcher or as artillery tractors to tow 57mm anti-tank guns.

LIGHT/MEDIUM TANKS

Designed and built alongside the T-26 series was the BT, Fast Tank series based upon the American M 1931 Christie Convertible Tank, two of which had been purchased from the United States in 1932, then minutely inspected and tested by Russian tank designers. At 10.5tons, they were light enough to be classified in the light tank category, but were really designed as medium tanks.

First of the series was the BT-1 (BT: *Bystrochodya* – fast tank) which was very similar in many respects to the M1931; even the engine was a copy of the original Liberty. It was armed with two machine guns but had little armour, making it clearly inadequate as a fighting vehicle and production ceased after only a few had been built. The BT-2 was developed and was similar, except that it had a new turret with a 37mm gun and a ball-mounted MG. Built in late 1931, it went into full production the following year. The BT-3 & BT-4 were both improvements on the same design. BT-3 had solid disc-type road wheels instead of spoked and now mounted a 45mm gun. Both were produced in limited numbers. In 1937, a bridgelayer version of the BT-3 was also built.

The first major production model was the BT-5, which had a larger, cylindrical turret for the 45mm gun, a new engine and stronger suspension. There was also a close support version BT-5A mounting a 76.2mm howitzer, as well as the usual commander's version - BT-5(V). The BT-5 was in service at the outbreak of war and had superior firepower and mobility over many of its contemporaries.

Next to appear, in 1935, was the BT-7 series. BT-7-2 had a new semi-conical-shaped turret, thicker armour and was of all-welded construction. The BT-7 was deployed in considerable numbers and several were captured and re-deployed by both the Finns and Germans. The BT-7M of 1939 had to be virtually re-designed, so as to be able to take the V-2 diesel engine, which gave it a top speed of over 40mph and a range of 375 miles, using jettisonable fuel tanks. It also had a very different sloping front glacis instead of the pointed nose which had been a major recognition feature of the series. The gun was now a 76.2mm.

Specifications	BT-1	BT-5	BT-7	BT-IS
Weight (tons)	10.2	11.5	13.8	15.6
Crew	three	three	three	three
Dimensions				
Length:	18ft	18ft	18ft 7ins	19ft
Width:	7ft 4ins	7ft 4ins	8ft	7ft 6ins
Height:	6ft 4ins	7ft 3ins	7ft 6ins	7ft 6ins
Armour				
thickness	6-13mm	6-13mm	6-22mm	6-30mm
Armament	two MG	45mm	45mm	45mm
		one MG	two MG	one MG
Engine	400hp	350hp	450hp	500hp
		all petrol engines		
Top speed	40-70mph	40-70mph	45mph	40mph

Final model of the BT series was the BT-IS, which was built as a prototype only, and based upon BT-7M, but had sloping armour both at the

front and on the sides. The turret was still semi-conical and mounted a 45mm gun. The 15.6ton tank is important even though it was only built as a prototype, because its direct descendant was the famous T-34.

The design team then began work on a replacement for the BT and produced a wooden mock-up of a tank known as the A-20. This design followed strictly the requirements laid down by General Pavlov, then head of the Directorate of Armoured Forces (ABTU), who had specified an agile tank, with 20mm armour, a 45mm gun, still convertible from wheels to tracks. The design team were most unhappy, arguing that battle experience (in Spain) had shown that the convertible requirement was both useless and unnecessary, that the tank should have armour at least 30mm thick and that a 76mm gun was required to defeat known potential enemy tanks. It is rumoured that Stalin personally attended their presentation and gave his permission for the heavier prototype to be built, in addition to A-20. Originally called A-30 it was later designated T-32.

MEDIUM TANKS

Various models of multi-turreted Exploitation tanks were built, both in the medium and heavy classes, being the Red Army's answer to the German Nbz, British A1E1 (Independent) and French *Char de Rupture*. The T-28 weighed some 27.5tons, had a 76.2mm gun (the prototype only had a 45mm) in the main turret and two separate MG turrets. It was 18ft long, 9ft 2ins wide, 9ft 3ins high and had armour 10-30mm thick, a crew of six and was powered by a 500hp engine, allowing a top speed of 23mph.

It was used in the Russo-Finnish War, as were the heavy tank versions. The T-28A was an improved production model, with thicker front armour, whilst T-28(V) was the usual commander's model, complete with frame aerial. Most of the next model, the T-28B, were armed with the longer, more powerful, 76.2mm L/26 gun, which also had a turret basket and better vision areas for the driver. Final model was the T-28C, which had thicker armour - up to 80mm on the front of the tank and high armour screens around the turret which mounted a L/26 gun. The T-28C was first used against the Panzerwaffe in 1941. The Soviets did convert a small number of T-28s to carry flamethrowers, designated OT-28. There was also a bridgelaying version, IT-28. Production ceased in 1940.

Both the light/medium tank prototypes, A-20 and T-32 (A-30), were taken to the test grounds at Kubinka in July 1939 for exhaustive trials and two months later a special display was

Above: **A Soviet T-70 light tank passing a knocked-out German PzKpfw IV during the crushing of the German summer offensive of 1943, in the Orel-Kursk region.** *(GF)*

Above left: **This T-26 Soviet light tank is in the colours of the Finnish Army, 1939-40. It was donated to the Tank Museum by Finland in 1990.** *(TM)*

Far left: **KV-1B, was developed in 1941. To counter German short range anti-tank weapons additional armour was fitted.** *(TM)*

Left: **T-34, one of the best tanks of World War Two and probably the best medium tank of its generation.** *(TM)*

Right and below:
The all-round excellence of the T-34 came as something of a shock to the Germans and led directly to the rapid design and building of Panther. Over 40,000 of all Marks of T-34 were built during the war and of those 12,000 were the T34/85. Its powerful armament, sleek lines, good cross-country performance and reliability, made it an excellent medium tank. It still had difficulty knocking out the heavier German Panzers, but could hold its own against PzKpfw III and IV. This well restored T34/85 is being driven over the training area at the Royal Armoured Corps Centre, Bovington, Dorset. *(TM)*

Right: **One of the best tanks of all time, the T-34/76, this is the 76B model, with the long-barrelled version of the 76.2mm L/40 gun.** *(TM)*

held featuring all the Red Army's new tanks, for the Main Military Council (GVS). These included both the A-20 and T-32 mediums, the T-40 and T-50 lights and the new KV heavy. The head of the design group for medium tanks, M I Koshkin, argued that the T-32 should be capable of performing the same tasks of not only the BT fast series but also the T-26 infantry support tank and the T-28 medium. No final decision was made as Pavlov still favoured the A-20. It required a further meeting in December 1940 to make the final vital decision, which was heavily influenced by the way the Finnish anti-tank guns had dealt with Russian armour and the inability of the 45mm gun to damage bunkers. It was shown by Koshkin that the T-32 was able to be up-armoured as necessary and the Defence Committee finally agreed to the building of such a tank. Designated T-34, it was to prove one of the best tanks of World War Two.

Specifications	A-20	T-32	T-34/76A
Weight (tons)	19.8	19	26.3
Crew	four	four	four
Dimensions			
Length:	17ft 9ins	17ft 9ins	21ft 7ins
Width:	8ft 9ins	8ft 9ins	9ft 9ins
Height:	7ft 9ins	7ft 9ins	8ft 0ins
Armour thickness	15-60mm	30-60mm	14-45mm
Armament	45mm gun	76.2mm gun all two MG	76.2mm gun
Engine *a*	450hp	450hp all diesel	500hp
Top speed	40mph	38mph	31mph

Note *a*. The V-2 engine was a V-12 water-cooled diesel, perfected in 1936 (the world's first purpose designed tank deisel engine) and trialled in the BT 5 fast tank in 1939. Powerful and economical, it was uprated to 500bhp at 1,800 rpm for the T-34, and for the KV heavy tank, uprated to 600bhp at 2,000rpm.

The first T-34 left the assembly line at the Kharkov plant in June 1940, the prototypes having been under stringent testing since the end of 1939. Series production was carried out at a number of factories, initially at Kharkov, Leningrad and Stalingrad. Then, when the Germans surrounded Leningrad and pushed into the Ukraine, the Leningrad and Kharkov factories had to be moved to a safer location at Chelyabinsk behind the Ural Mountains. Here they amalgamated with an existing tractor factory to form the Soviets' largest tank engineering site - known as Tankograd. The Stalingrad factory kept up production even when the enemy was at its very gates. It is said that T-34s were driven straight off the assembly lines out of the factory, unpainted and even in some cases not completely finished, to go into battle with the Panzers.

The T-34 made its first combat appearance in the summer of 1941, its reasonably thick angled armour, hard hitting 76.2mm gun and excellent mobility putting it in a class above its German contemporaries, the PzKpfw III and IV. This came as a great shock to the Germans and, as we shall see, forced them to embark upon a costly and urgent improvement programme in order to up-armour, up-gun their existing Panzers and most importantly to produce Panther. Also the T-34 could be fitted with a rudimentary form of Schnorkel gear allowing the crossing of water obstacles. In 1944, T-34s (plus some T-44s) were used in the crossings of Rivers Bug and Vistula.

Left: **T-34s and infantry advance by fire and movement across open ground. The T-34 was produced in six models (A to F) before the up-gunned and re-designated T34/85.** *(GF)*

A number of models of T-34/76 were produced during the war, the main types being:

T-34/76A: initial production model.

T-34/76B: second production model, incorporating rolled-plate turret, mounting a new 76.2mm L/40 gun. Late production models had a cast turret and all-steel wheels (due to the rubber shortage), increasing weight to 28 tons.

T-34/76C: third production model, with larger turret (two hatches instead of one), better tracks, better vision devices and an armoured sleeve for the hull MG. Weight now 30 tons, top speed 30mph.

T-34/76D: fourth production model, with new hexagonal-shaped turret and wide gun mantlet. Jettisonable fuel tanks, allowing extra range. Weight now 30.9 tons, with armour up to 70mm and a top speed of 31mph.

T-34/76E: as for D, but of all-welded construction, with a commander's cupola and better engine cooling.

T-34/76F: as for D, but with cast turret, five-speed gearbox. Only 100 built, then production switched to T-34/85.

In addition, there were the usual commanders tanks and some flame conversions. The ATO 41 was based on the T-34/76B and ATO-42 (OT-34) based on T-34/76D, which had double the flame fuel capacity. Both had the flamegun in place of the hull MG. The T-34 was also used, like Sherman, as a basis to add on specialised equipment such as mine-rollers, to convert to ARV and bridgelayer, and even to develop a medium artillery transporter, although this got no further than the prototype stage. Models included:

TT-34: without turret, equipped with a boom and winch, used as a mobile crane or an ARV. Weight was 30 tons

T-34-MTU: bridgelayer, with a rigid bridge, launched by pivoting about a roller fixed to the front. Other bridges included an A type and a scissors-type, also improvised wooden bridges were sometimes used, as were fascines and various types of matting.

T-34-PT34: mine rollers pushed by T-34. Other mine-clearing equipment included Snake explosive filled hoses either pushed or projected across a minefield, then exploded to make gaps.

T-34-STU: tank-dozer fitted with a manual/hydraulic operated blade.

Other improvements. A much improved T-34/76D was needed to fight the German Tiger and its 88mm gun, this required increasing frontal armour up to 110mm. Designated T-43, it was similar to the D model except its length was now 22ft 6ins, armour was 18-110mm thick, and it weighed 31.5 tons Only a few were produced because of the entry into service of the up-gunned T-34/85. Operations against the

Above: **A late model T-34/76F, fitted with Mugalev mine rollers, designed to help engineer units to clear paths through enemy minefields. Each roller could withstand some 8-10 detonations from exploding anti-tank mines. The special tanks were known as PT-34s and were successfully used on the Eastern Front.** *(TM)*

Above: **The T-35 heavy tank weighed 45 tons, the main turret mounting a 76.2mm howitzer, while two of the four sub-turrets had 37mm guns and two machine guns. Shown is the commander's version in a parade on Red Square, Moscow.** *(TM)*

heavier German Panthers and Tigers, had shown that the Soviets needed a gun with a longer range and better penetration. After a great deal of work and trials, the 85mm ZiS-S-53 gun, designed by F Grabin, was chosen. This was based, like the German 88mm, on a current AA gun. The turret was a modified version from the KV-85. In 1944 T-34/85 entered service and production continued long after the war had ended.

Specifications	T34/85	T-44
Weight (tons)	31.5	31 to 34 (depending on gun)
Crew	four	four
Dimensions		
Length:	24ft 7ins	25ft (or 26ft 6ins) (depending on gun)
Width:	9ft 8ins	10ft 2ins
Height:	7ft 8ins	7ft 9ins
Armour		
thickness	18–75mm	15–120mm
Armament	85mm one MG	85mm or 100mm two MG
Engine (diesel)	500hp	512hp
top speed	31mph	32mph

The table above compares it with the last Soviet medium tank of the war, the T-44, which entered production in 1945. This was a total redesign of the T-34, with a lower silhouette, torsion-bar suspension, enlarged turret and

thicker armour. Later models had a 100mm gun instead of the 85mm. It was only produced in limited numbers due to mechanical problems and was replaced, post-war, by the T-54 series.

Over 40,000 of all T-34 variants were produced during the Great Patriotic War and it was undoubtedly the most important tank in the Red Army, lending itself to mass production and proving its battlefield superiority. However, it did have problems, one of the main ones being the two man turret, while battlefield control was difficult due to a shortage of radios (none below platoon commander level). The low turret, although reducing the overall silhouette, meant that the gun would not depress more than three degrees, which led to difficulties when engaging close-range targets, or firing from hull-down positions. There was also little in the way of crew comfort. More importantly, T-34 was really not a match for the German Tiger. 'The T-34 raises it's hat whenever it meets a Tiger', was the way that German soldiers described the 88mm armour-piercing shot ripping the turret completely off a T-34 and hurling it several yards away.

HEAVY TANKS

In 1932, a requirement arose for a heavy tank capable of dealing with enemy infantry and anti-tank weapons (like the French Char 2C) and over

Left: **The KV-1 was based closely on the T-100/SMK heavy tanks, but with only one turret, mounting a 76.2mm L/40 gun. There were a number of versions, weighing from 46 to 47 tons, depending upon armour thickness. This is a KV-1B, which had extra armour on the front and sides.**

the next seven years various models of first the T-32, then T-35 heavy tanks were produced. Weighing around 45 tons, they were well armed with a 76.2mm howitzer in the main turret, four subsidiary turrets, two of which (offside front and nearside rear) mounted 45mm guns, while the other two had MGs.

Specifications	T-32	T-35
Weight (tons)	44.8	45
Crew	ten	ten
Dimensions		
Length:	30ft 6ins	31ft 6ins
Width:	10ft 6ins	10ft 6ins
Height:	10ft	11ft 3ins
Armour		
thickness	11–25mm	11–35mm
Armament	76.2mm gun,	76.2mm gun,
	two 37mm guns	two 45mm
	six MG	six MG
Engine (petrol)	345hp	500hp
Top speed	18mph	18mph

A few were fitted with flamethrowers, and also the normal commander's models, with their conspicuous radio aerials (only platoon commanders and above had radios). Some saw action in the Russo-Finnish War and again during Operation Barbarossa, where many were destroyed.

The T-100, designed as the replacement for T-35, was again multi-turreted, but this time with only two turrets, 76.2mm gun (top) and a 45mm gun (bottom). These also saw combat in Finland, but were found to be too large and difficult to manoeuvre The project was dropped in 1940 in favour of the KV series. Alongside the T-100, another multi-turreted tank appeared in 1937. The SMK heavy tank (named after the Soviet political leader Sergei Mironovich Kirov, assassinated in 1934) like the T-100, was a complete departure from usual Soviet design. The hull had eight suspension wheels on each side, with torsion-bar suspension and four return rollers. It suffered the same fate as the T-100.

Below: **The KV-2A was the close support version mounting a 152mm howitzer in a large, slab-sided turret . It weighed 53 tons.** *(TM)*

Specifications	T-100	SMK
Weight (tons)	56	45
Crew	seven	seven
Dimensions		
Length:	29ft 4ins	31ft 6ins
Width:	9ft 9ins	10ft 6ins
Height:	10ft 9ins	10ft 6ins
Armour thickness	30-60mm	30-60mm
Armament	Both 76.2mm and 45mm gun	
	and three MG	
Engine (petrol)	400hp	400hp
Top speed	18.75mph	20mph

Below : **IS-2, the improved version of the IS-1, was the major production model, 2,250 being built. Photographed near the Brandenburg Gate, Berlin, 1945.** *(GF)*

Headed by Lieutenant-Colonel Kotin, the heavy tank design team did not like the twin-turret design of the T-100 and SMK, but managed to get Stalin's permission to develop a single turreted version of SMK, which they named KV after Klimenti Voroshilov, Defence Commissar and at the time, friend of Stalin. The new tank was to have mounted an up-dated version of the 76.2mm gun, but this was not immediately available. In September 1939, the KV outperformed both T-100 and SMK during trials at Kubinka, then the prototypes were sent north for combat trials during the Winter War. It performed well, although one KV prototype was damaged and photographed by the Finns – fortunately German experts identified it as a T-35. At the same time as designing the normal KV mounting a 76.2mm gun, the team worked on a heavier version would be able carry a 152mm howitzer in a larger turret, so as to be more able to destroy enemy bunkers. The two types were initially known as KV small turret and KV large turret, but were then designated as KV-1 and KV-2.

The KV-1 was produced in various versions. The KV-1A was the improved 1940 model, with the L/40 gun and new mantlet. The KV-1B of 1941 was up-armoured, with 25-35mm of additional metal on the front of the hull and the sides, plus extra armour bolted to the turret. Produced in 1942, the KV-1C had an improved, cast turret, thicker armour (now up to 120mm) a more powerful (600hp) engine and wider tracks, all of which increased weight to 47 tons. Between 1942 and 1943 two other versions were produced in small numbers, the KV-1S (S: *Skorostnoy* - fast),

with less armour (only up to 60mm), weighed only 42.5tons and had a top speed of 25mph. There was also a version which mounted the 85mm gun in a larger, cast turret and weighed 46 tons.

The KV-2 appeared in two versions, the KV-2A of 1940, which mounted the 152mm howitzer, although some of the early models had a 122mm howitzer. It proved to be unwieldy and was replaced by the KV-2B, which was an improved version on the KV-1B chassis, had a better mantlet, was 4 tons heavier and 18 inches higher.

Specifications	KV-1	KV-2
Weight (tons)	46.35	53
Crew	five	six
Dimensions		
Length:	22ft 7ins	22ft 4ins
Width:	10ft 7ins	10ft 9ins
Height:	8ft 9ins	12ft
Armour thickness	30-75mm	35-100mm
Armament	76.2mm gun	152mm howitzer
	three MG	two MG
Engine (diesel)	550hp	550hp
Top speed	22mph	16mph

During the summer of 1943, Kotin's design team had been working on various new versions of the KV, incorporating new turrets, suspension and hull layouts. One of these became known as the IS-1 (IS: *Ioseph Stalin* - Joseph Stalin) or IS-85 as it mounted an 85mm gun. The change from KV to IS came about because Voroshilov was now in disgrace - in fact he had been so

since the débâcle following the German invasion, (Dmitry Pavlov had been liquidated!). Around 100 plus IS-85s were built in the autumn of 1943, but later models were armed firstly with the 100mm gun and then the 122mm, designated IS-100 and IS-122. Firing trials took place at Kubinka in late 1943, a captured Panther being used as the target. An observer noted '... a 122mm round crashed through the frontal armour and clear through the rear armour as well.' The 100mm gun had an even better performance, but there was spare 122mm production capacity and also adequate ammunition supply, whereas the availability of the 100mm was extremely erratic, so the 122mm gun was chosen. After its battlefield debut in April 1944, the new tank was in great demand.

The improved model, IS-2 became the main production model, 2,250 being built. Its front glacis was more streamlined, but nowhere near as much as the entire body of the next model, the IS-3, a complete redesign. Its low silhouette, graceful lines and firepower made it the most advanced heavy tank of its time.

Soviet heavy tanks were improved immeasurably during the Great Patriotic War, the multi-turreted T-100 and SMK being totally outdated in comparison with the sleek lines of the IS-3. Not only was there a vast increase in weapon hitting power, but also to the armour thickness on turrets and front glacis, which gave the heavy tanks almost total battlefield immunity, except from one of their own kind.

Far left: **The KV-85 was produced in 1943 and mounted an 85mm gun in a larger cast turret than that of the KV-1, increasing its battle weight to 46 tons.** *(TM)*

Below: **Probably the most advanced heavy tank of its time, the IS-3 known as the 'Pike'. The powerful 122mm gun, thick armour (up to 120mm) and low silhouette, made it a battle winner.** *(GF)*

CHAPTER SIX

France

'You cannot hope to achieve real breakthroughs with tanks.
The tank is not independent enough. It has to go ahead, but then
must return for fuel and supplies.'

General Maurice Gamelin, French Chief of Staff and Supreme Commander of all French land forces, 1939.

Like Great Britain, France had made considerable use of tanks during World War One, with Colonel (later General) Jean Baptiste Estienne matching Swinton, Elles and Fuller's crusading zeal for the new weapon. The French built thousands of tanks, probably more than anyone else, especially the small, light Renault FT 17 which they used mainly to support infantry, while their *Artillerie d'Assaut* used the larger Schneider and St Chamond, as the name implies as assault artillery. After World War One, Estienne continued to crusade for mechanised forces with the tank as the most essential equipment while another tank enthusiast, General Aime Doumenc, also proposed the formation of complete armoured divisions. Unfortunately, Marshal Petain had never been particularly impressed by tanks during the war and saw them only as a useful adjunct to the infantry. Although there was no wholesale disbandment of tank units as in Britain and the United States, French tanks were made an integral part of the infantry in 1920 and the *Artillerie d'Assaut* organisation disbanded.

Although mass of outdated armour was kept in service - one estimate of the number FT 17s still operational in 1921 was over 3,700 - an effort was made to modernise them, for example by fitting new running gear (made by Citroen-Kegresse) tested in the mid-1920s but without conclusive results. In 1925, tanks were sent to assist in crushing a rebellion in Morocco.

With no new tactics being developed for their use they remained just an addition to the infantry, with some plus points, but not to be taken too seriously especially as the French 'grand design' was based upon strong defences whilst the tank was seen as an offensive weapon.

In 1925, the French War Ministry decided to adopt a policy of producing three types of tanks - light, medium and heavy, the last category including super heavy. In the lightest of these categories was the proposed successor to the FT 17, the Char NC 1 built by Renault (also known as the NC 27) this was essentially an up-armoured version of the FT 17 with improved suspension. It did not enter service but a few were sold to Japan. The NC 2 (also known as NC 31) followed this and had a more powerful engine, but was again rejected by the French Army and sold instead to Greece. At the other end of the scale was the 68-ton Char 2C – *Char de Rupture* – breakthrough tank, designed during World War One for use in the large scale offensive planned for 1919 but did not become operational until 1921. It was the first multi-turreted tank in the world and had a crew of twelve, but it was far too large and cumbersome. The disarmament conferences of the period did little to justify its further development.

When France did start to mechanise in the mid-1930s and begin to build more modern, better armoured and better armed AFVs, some of the FT 17s remained in service and were still

there even well into World War Two. For example, FT 17s were used by the Vichy French against the Americans during the Operation Torch landings in North Africa, November 1942.

However, the new French tanks of the 1930s were among the best in the world and quite capable of holding their own against any opposition. Nevertheless, the French continued to see the tank merely as a support weapon and felt that their decision not to have independent armoured formations was totally vindicated by the tank's apparently poor showing against anti-tank guns in the Spanish Civil War.

Edouard Daladier, the French Minister of National Defence in 1937 claimed: 'The Spanish Civil War has seen the crumbling of immense hopes based on certain machines... Outside Madrid, the tanks lay pierced like sieves'.

Of course there were dissenting voices, one of the strongest being that of Charles de Gaulle, then a Colonel, who wrote a short pamphlet *Vers l'armee de metier* (Towards a professional army) in 1934. In this he set out his ideas for a properly established armoured division and distributed copies to such armoured enthusiasts as Estienne and Doumenc, also outside of France. Petain was furious and struck him off the promotion list of 1936, ensuring that de Gaulle would remain in obscurity until World War Two. De Gaulle would however, get the opportunity to prove his theories, albeit when it was far too late to have any real effect upon the enemy.

At the start of World War Two, France had a large armoured force, probably one of the best - if not the best - in the world, which was made up of some extremely good tanks and supporting AFVs. Unfortunately, their tactical thinking remained firmly in the past and the majority of these tanks were dispersed in small units and not concentrated into armoured divisions. By the time they had awakened to the danger and formed *Divisions Légère Mécanique* (DLM) these units lacked offensive power, while their other armoured formation *Division Cuirassée* (DCR), lacked both reconnaissance potential and mobility. They would all prove to be easily defeated by the Blitzkrieg tactics of the Panzerwaffe.

The French tanks which fought in France, 1940 had of course mainly been built in the period 1935 to 1940 with no further tank production taking place, so it is useful to summarise the number of tanks in service in France, May 1940.

Type		
Light tanks	– under 15 tons	2,720
Medium tanks	– 15 to 25 tons	400
Heavy tanks	– over 25 tons	300
	TOTAL	3,470

Of this total, 1,100 were armed with at least 37mm guns

Above: **A column of Char Leger Renault R 35 light infantry support tanks moving across country. In May 1940 over 1,400 Char Legers were in service.** *(TM)*

Right: **The Char Leger AMR 35, also known as the AMR ZT, was fitted with suspension which became the standard pattern for French light tanks. This version mounts the 25mm gun.** *(TM)*

Below: **Char Leger FCM 36 infantry tank. The octagonal turret mounted a 37mm gun. About 100 of those built saw action in 1940.** *(TM)*

INFANTRY & CAVALRY TANKS

Just as with the US Army, there was a distinction made between tanks to support the infantry and tanks and armoured cars which would be built to equip the mechanised cavalry (this had begun in the early 1930s). The cavalry vehicles were known as *Auto-mitrailleuses* (machine-gun cars) and were of three types:

AMR *(Auto-Mitrailleuse de Reconnaissance)* - light tanks, armed with a machine gun(s) and capable of cross-country reconnaissance.
AMC *(Auto-Mitrailleuse de Combat)* - heavier tanks, better armed and armoured which could fight for information.
AMD *(Auto-Mitrailleuse de Decouverte)* - long-range reconnaissance vehicles, normally armoured cars.

The main *Chars de Cavalerie* were the Hotchkiss H 35 and H 39, also the Somua S 35 and S 40.

The infantry tanks were designated *Chars* and comprised four types, within the light, medium and heavy classifications.
Chars Légers – light tanks, under 15 tons armed with 37mm gun and a 7.5mm MG – Renault R 35, and R 40; FCM 36 and Hotchkiss H 35.
Chars Moyens – medium tanks, 15 to 25 tons armed with 47mm gun and several MGs; Renault D 1 and D 2 and Somua S35.
Chars de Battaille – battle tanks, over 25 tons, armed with larger than a 47mm gun but lighter than the super-heavy tanks. Strictly speaking, these were also part of the *Chars Lourds* heavy tank type – Renault B1 and B1bis.
Chars Lourds – heavy tanks over 60 tons and were strictly speaking, super heavy – the Char 2C

Not all the French Army's tanks fought in France, May 1940 some were overseas – FT 17s in Morocco – whilst others were in development or just beginning production (AMX 38, only a few were completed by late 1939, then the project was terminated in 1940).

LIGHT TANKS

The 5.5-ton light tank AMR-VM (also called the AMR 33) was the first model to appear in 1933, and was only called 'AMR' to disguise the fact that it was being supplied to the cavalry. Armed with a single 7.5mm machine gun operated by a crew of two, it had armour only 13mm thick and a top speed of 30mph. It had unusual suspension with a twin-wheeled bogie in the centre which was free to pivot about the lower end of a vertical coil-spring, with two more single bogies on right-angle arms in front

Above: **This version of the AMR 35 light tank mounted a 13.2mm machine gun instead of the 25mm cannon. Around 200, AMR 35s were built and widely used.** *(TM)*

and behind. The upper ends of the arms were interconnected by a system of springs and bellcrank levers - an over elaborate arrangement which was never again used.

The AMR-VM was followed by the AMR-ZT (also called the AMR 35) and was very similar but mounted either a 25mm gun or one 13.2mm and one 7.5mm MG. The other major difference was the suspension, the coil-springs being replaced by thick rubber washers and the centre pair of road wheels mounted on bell-cranks. This became the standard pattern suspension for French light tanks. A total of 120 AMR-VM and 200 AMR-ZT were in service in May 1940. Another version, the AMC Renault YB was an AMR chassis with R35 light tank turret and was intended for use as a cavalry tank but was never produced in any quantity.

The Renault R 35 light infantry support tank weighed nearly 10 tons had a two-man crew and mounted a 37mm gun plus co-ax MG in a cast turret with a cupola and an armoured jacket over the armament. It appeared in 1935, as the replacement for the FT 17 and had armour up to 45mm thick. In 1938, a variant of the R 35 was produced in small numbers which mounted a longer 37mm gun but had the same four-cylinder, 82hp Renault engine. The last version was the R 40 which weighed between 10 and 11 tons, mounted the longer gun and had a detachable tail-skid to improve ditch crossing but was otherwise very similar to the R 35. By May 1940 a total of 1400, R 35 and R40 tanks were in service.

The H 35 closely resembled the R 35 externally and had the same armament but thinner armour (12-34mm). The two-man tank was powered by a six-cylinder Hotchkiss engine and had a top speed of 17.5mph. This was followed into service by the H 39, mounting a

Above: The Renault AMC 35 light tank (also known as the ACGI) mounted a 47mm gun and weighed 14.5 tons. (TM)

Right: A Char S 35 Somua medium tank being chained down on a railway flatcar by French workmen. The Somua was one of the best French tanks, being better than most of its German contemporaries. Captured S 35s were used by both German and Italian forces. (TM)

longer (1938 pattern) 37mm gun without an armoured jacket. Both Hotchkiss models used basically the same type of suspension as the Renaults but with three, twin-wheeled bogies and two return rollers in place of the three on the Renault. The H 39 (also known as the H 40) had a more powerful 120hp engine which increased its top speed to 22.5mph. Around 900, H 35 and H 39 were in service May, 1940.

In terms of armour and armament, the H 35 and R 35 were better equipped than their Panzer equivalents, but they only carried a two-man crew, whereas PzKpfw IIA for example had a three-man crew. As any tank crewman knows, this extra man makes all the difference when in action on the battlefield.

The Char FCM36, built by the Societe des Forges et Chantiers de la Mediterraneé in 1936 was a 12-ton light infantry support tank mounting a 37mm gun and MG in an octagonal-shaped turret, which had a non-rotating command post at the back. The chassis had

prominent mud chutes along the top run of the tracks. The suspension system was made up of nine grouped pairs of wheels, a single at the front and all controlled by helical springs. The 90hp Berliet diesel engine gave the tank a top speed of 15mph. A total of only 100 were produced.

MEDIUM TANKS

The Char D tank built by Renault was, together with a few Char Bs, the only new tank to come into French Army service between 1918 and 1935. Based on the NC 27, the Char D 1A appeared in 1931 as a 12-ton tank with a crew of three and mounting a 37mm gun plus two MGs (one co-ax). It had a top speed of 12 mph and armour 14-30mm thick. The next model, D 1B, mounted a 47mm and weighed 14 tons - mainly due to thicker armour (now up to 40mm). Its more powerful engine (100hp instead of 64hp) allowed it a top speed of 12.5mph. Most Char D 1s were deployed in North Africa so did not see action on the home front in 1940.

The Char D 2 which was considerably heavier - 20 tons, had a six-cylinder 150hp engine which allowed a top speed of 20mph. It was fitted with a cast turret which had rounded corners (like the R35). Superstructure panniers were built over the tracks and it had higher back decking than the D1. The same strange suspension as the D1 was still used with twenty-four wheels on each side, in two different sizes. The larger ones being used singly, while the smaller wheels were grouped into two or three-wheeled bogies controlled by coil-springs. This did not allow for a very smooth ride. Only fifty D2s were built.

Below: **The Char D2 medium infantry tank had armour 40mm thick, a cast turret but an almost vertical front hull face.** *(TM)*

Right: **The Char 2C *Char du Rupture*, was designed in World War One but did not enter service until 1935. The last six of these 68-ton tanks were supposed to have been destroyed by enemy air attack on the way to the front line in May, 1940. This is one of those tanks being examined by German troops and appears undamaged.** *(TM)*

The Somua S35, developed from the D 1 and D 2 retained the same one-man turret (as fitted to the D 20) but had a crew of three, weighed 20 tons and mounted a long barrelled 47mm gun with a 7.5mm co-ax MG. The clamshell-type cast hull had upper and lower parts joined by bolts, but it was well armoured (20-55mm) and had good performance with a top speed of 25mph. However the one-man turret detracted from its fightability, although it was one of the best medium tanks of the period. It was the first French tank with a cast hull and turret, but was vulnerable to German Panzers. Around 400, S 35s were in service in France, May 1940.

HEAVY TANKS

In 1918, when General Estienne had advocated the building of a 15-ton tank mounting a 75mm gun, the Char B was the ultimate development of this proposal. It was designed in the 1920s but the first prototypes did not appear until 1932, when extra armour was requested and speed and cross-country performance had to be improved. The Char B 1 came into service in 1935, it weighed 31 tons had a crew of four and was armed with 37mm gun and co-ax MG in a turret - the first French tank to have electric-power traverse in addition to normal hand operated traverse. Mounted in the hull next to the driver was a short-barrelled 75mm howitzer, which could not be traversed so had to be aimed by tracking the tank. To assist in this manoeuvre a double differential was fitted with a Naeder hydrostatic pump-drive in the auxiliary drive-shaft from the gearbox, allowing an infinitely graduated series of turning radii in each gear. With armour 14-60mm thick and a six-cylinder 270hp engine, the tank had a power-to-weight ratio (hp/ton) of only 8.7 and a top speed of 17.5mph.

A second version, Char B1bis, weighed 32 tons had a more powerful 300hp engine which improved the hp/ton ratio to 9.4, giving the tank a better cross-country performance. It also had a 47mm gun fitted in the turret in place of the 37mm. The third version B1ter, weighed 34 tons had a more powerful 350hp engine and its hull-mounted 75mm howitzer now had five degrees of traverse. Only five B1ter were built but in total there were 300-320 Char B in service by 1940 mainly with in the DCR.

During World War One a specification had been issued for a heavy breakthrough tank – a *Char de Rupture* weighing about 40 tons. Two prototypes Char 1A and 1B had been built between 1917 and 1918. Later development then produced an even heavier model, the Char

2 C at nearly 70 tons, and a massive 33ft 8ins long, 9ft 8ins high and 13ft 8ins wide. Ten were built and delivered in 1922, it being then the most powerful tank in the world. The Char 2C had a crew of twelve, mounted a 75mm in the front turret and four MGs (one in a separate turret at the rear). A single model was converted to mount a 155mm howitzer as well as the 75mm. Power was provided by two six-cylinder 250hp Mercedes engines (reparations from Germany). Despite their size and apparent invulnerability, the superheavy breakthrough tanks were destined not to see any action. In 1940, the remaining six where being moved up to the front by rail, when most were destroyed by enemy air attack. (see caption page 182).

After the surrender of France in May 1940 some captured French tanks were pressed into service by the Germans for use in occupied France and elsewhere (Channel Islands). Others saw combat on the Eastern Front and in Finland under German designations:

PzKpfw B-2 740(f) - Char B1bis - some used as flamethrowers with a flamegun replacing the 75mm howitzer.

PzKpfw 35-S 739(f) - Somua S 35 - despite its one-man turret this was considered to be the best French tank by the Panzerwaffe and was first used by them in combat in Finland, June 1941.

PzKpfw 38H 735(f) - Hotchkiss H 35, H 38 & H 39 - As Somua they were used in Finland, 1941 also Norway and the Balkans.

PzKpfw 35R 731(f) - Renault R 35 - garrison duties in France and the Channel Islands.

Far left: **The 32 ton Char B1bis heavy tank evolved from the B1 but was up-armoured to 60mm. The hull mounted 75mm howitzer had a limited amount of traverse.** *(TM)*

Below: **This version of the R35 is equipped with a fascine carrier. The fascine was dropped into a ditch or trench to facilitate crossing. Some were used in 1940.** *(TM)*

CHAPTER SEVEN

Italy

'Armoured troops played a negligible part in Italian campaigns up to a fairly recent date. Armoured formations did not appear until 1938.'

Brief Notes on the Italian Army, from GHQ Middle East Forces, August 1942

Although the Italians were among the first countries to show interest in armoured fighting vehicles - their armoured car, the Isotta-Fraschini Tipo RM appearing in 1911 – they showed little interest in tanks at the outbreak of war. Perhaps it was that their area of the World War One battlefields did not lend itself to the deployment of armour, being in the main far too mountainous. They did experiment in some tank design (Fiat 2000 - two built in 1917), but in the end contented themselves by copying the ubiquitous Renault FT17, which they designated the Fiat 3000.

The first Italian tank unit comprised the only two 40-ton Fiat 2000, plus six Renaults. After 1921, this unit was renamed as an independent tank company and re-equipped with Fiat 3000, but no further developments took place for the next seven years. It was not until the Fascist dictator, Benito Mussolini came to power that tanks started to be taken more seriously.

Italy began by purchasing four Carden-Loyd tankettes in 1929, then copying them to build a further twenty-one at the Fiat-Ansaldo works in Genoa, and designated CV-29 (*Carro Veloce* 29). At the same time they were producing an improved model of the Fiat 3000, which mounted a long-barrelled 37mm gun - a later model which appeared in 1936 had twin 37mm guns in the same turret. However, it was the CV-29 which interested them most of all, as they

felt that the 5-ton tankettes would be more suitable for use in mountainous terrain. This led to the first major build of AFVs by Ansaldo, namely of the CV-33 tankette. By World War Two, Italy had a fair number of tanks and had begun organising and equipping armoured divisions, embracing the philosophy that tanks should be used aggressively. Their armoured warfare manual of 1940, states that tanks should be deployed: 'offensively, in mass and by surprise'.

The Italians do not appear to have named their tank types but used the nomenclature: CA (*Carro Armato*) and CV (*Carro Veloce*) for tanks and tankettes, respectively, then adding two figures standing for the year in which it was designed.

Italian armour did of course see action prior to the start of World War Two, firstly in East Africa, where by April 1936 they had nearly 500 tanks/tankettes stationed. This force must have suffered some casualties during the annexation of Abyssinia. Secondly, in Spain where Italian 'volunteers', who fought for Franco, found that their lightly armoured tankettes were of little use against enemy anti-tank guns or the Soviet-built T-26 light tanks. A total of fifty-six tankettes were lost in Spain. The French also inflicted a number of casualties upon Italian armour when Mussolini launched an attack on 21 June 1940, against a handful of French Alpine divisions.

Up until 1940, the Italians had built 1,547 AFVs: 1,320 tankettes, twenty-seven light tanks

and one hundred mediums (M11/39). If one allows for the pre-war and 'invasion of France' casualties then it would appear that the Italians probably had some 1,300 to 1,400 tanks and tankettes in service when they started fighting the British in North Africa.

The subsequent heavy loss of tankettes made them stop building these ridiculous little machines and to start designing and producing heavier, better armed and armoured tanks. However, only a few had been completed by September 1939. There then followed four years of production, with self-propelled artillery guns being an increasingly larger part of manufacturing output.

Italy surrendered in September 1943, and no more tanks were built after that date, Germany seizing anything worthwhile, as well as recovering any remaining Stug IIIs, PzKpfw IIIs and IVs, twelve of each having been loaned to the Italians in 1943.

Although the Italians suffered tank casualties against the French in 1940, they were able to make use of captured French tanks (Somua and Renault R-35) supplied to them by Germany, for training and equipping units in Italy. Official Italian figures show that thirty-three Somua and 109, R-35s were pressed into Italian service in 1941, allowing their own manufactured tanks to be supplied to their forces fighting in North Africa - where they would all be destroyed or captured by the Allies.

Tank and SP gun production (all types) 1940-43

Year	Tanks	SP guns (Semoventi)
1940	235	-
1941	853	60
1942	475	195
1943	147	271
Total	1,710	526

Source: La Meccanizzazione Dell' Esercito Italiano Dalle Origini Al 1943 Volume One by Lucio Ceva and Andrea Curami.

TANKETTES & LIGHT TANKS

The Fiat Ansaldo L 3, the prototype of the CV-33, was itself derived from the CV-29 tankette and went through its final testing period in 1933. The initial order was for 1,300 vehicles, although more were eventually built as it was widely exported for example, to Albania, Austria, Bulgaria, Greece, Hungary, Nationalist Spain, Bolivia, Brazil and even to Afghanistan. Most of the export vehicles were standard production types, however, those going to the Afghans were armed with Danish-designed Madsen machine guns, and a special export model was sold to Brazil.

The 3.2-ton tankette had a crew of two, armour 5-15mm thick, mounted either one or two machine guns, was powered by a four-cylinder 43hp SPA CV-3 water-cooled petrol

Above: **L35 Lf, flamethrowers (***Carro Lanciaflamme***) in action. They towed an armoured 500 litre fuel trailer with a flamegun mounted in place of the tankette's normal machine gun(s).** *(TM)*

engine, which gave it a top speed of 26mph and a range of 78 miles. The CV-33 measured just 10ft 5ins long, by 4ft 7ins wide and 4ft 3ins high. Early hulls were riveted and welded, but later bolted contsruction was used. Those produced from 1938 had a modified stronger suspension, new tracks and better vision devices for the driver. A number of the older models were modified to this standard.

Some of the more modern vehicles were armed with a 20mm anti-tank gun, while numerous variants appeared:

L35/Lf - (Lf: *lanciaflamme*) flamethrower, with a flamegun, which had a range of approximately 100 metres replacing the MGs. It also towed a small trailer containing flame fuel, or mounted a fuel tank on the back of the tank.

CV-33 L35/r - command/radio tank, normally with armament removed to allow room for a map table and radios. It was fitted with a large hooped aerial stretching from front to rear over the turret.

CV-33/II (*Carro Veloce Passerella*) bridgelayer. A few of these specialised engineers vehicles were produced, also recovery vehicles, an AA tank and even a SP gun, but few saw action. In 1937, a light tank (the L 3)was built, using the CV-33

chassis on which was mounted a turret containing a 20mm automatic cannon. However, this light tank never entered production.

Although they strongly favoured the tankettes, the Italians did do some work on light tanks to replace them, the Fiat-Ansaldo 5 ton series of the mid-1930s being larger, heavier and better armed than the CV-33 although they were

used only for trials or training and did not see action. One of the models produced mounted a 37mm gun and this gave rise to the L 640 light tank series, which entered production in 1941. Various types were built with different armament, however, the production model mounted a 20mm Breda automatic gun and one MG and weighed just under 7 tons with armour 6-40mm thick. With a crew of only two (one man turret as the main armament was automatic), the 12ft 5ins long, 6ft 4ins wide and 6ft 8ins high vehicle was powered by a 70hp SPA 18D petrol engine which allowed it a top speed of 26mph and a range of 124 miles. Initially 280 were ordered with production starting in 1941, but this figure was reduced and many of those built were converted into the *Semovente* L 6/40 SP gun, by extending the superstructure, dispensing with the turret and fitting the 47mm Ansaldo 47/32 anti-tank gun. The resulting 6.4-ton tank destroyer was crewed by three men, working in very cramped conditions with poor vision devices. It was outclassed almost as soon as it entered service in North Africa.

MEDIUM TANKS

The M11/39 was an indifferent 11 ton, three-man, badly armoured and poorly armed medium tank and was out of date even before it first saw

Left: **The CV33 (*Carro Veloce*) was based upon the Vickers Carden-Loyd which the Italians were given a licence to manufacture from 1929 onwards. Various models of this 3.25-ton two-man tankette were produced over the years.** *(TM)*

action against the British in North Africa, 1940. Developed from the 8 ton CA light tank, which had also been another possible replacement for the CV-33 series, but was only produced as a prototype. Of riveted construction, and fitted with a rear-mounted V-8 105hp diesel engine it achieved a top speed of 21mph. The 15ft 6ins long M11 was just over 7ft wide and 7ft 4ins high. The turret was offset to the left and contained just twin-machine guns, while the 37mm main gun was in the chassis alongside the driver and operated by a gunner who sat beside him. In July 1940, of the 100 built seventy were sent to Libya but by January 1941 all had been destroyed or captured, as they were no match for the British Matilda II. Some of those captured were pressed into service by the Australians who used them with much more elan and dash than had their Italian crews. The M11/39 was eventually withdrawn in 1941.

Without doubt the best of the Italian tanks which followed the inferior M11/39 was the M 13/40, despite the fact that it was subject to mechanical breakdowns in the dusty desert conditions of North Africa, as it lacked engine sand filters and other desert modifications. It also had a disappointing cross-country performance and its bolted armour tended to split when struck by enemy fire, yet it was far superior to its

predecessor. The M13/40 had originally been conceived as a tank destroyer, armed with a 47mm gun and was based roughly on the M 11/39, the major difference being that the gun was now in a turret, and not the hull, allowing all-round traverse. The main gun was now properly manned as the crew had been increased to four men. More were built than any other Italian tank, 625 in total (including its successors) between 1940 and 1942. The first production models reached service units in Libya, 1940 and were used against the British. The first action was in the Sollum-Halfaya area 9 December, 1940.

M13/40		
Weight	14 tons	
Crew	four	
Dimensions	length:	16ft 2ins
	width:	7ft 3ins
	height:	7ft 10ins
Armour	14–40mm	
Armament	47mm gun and three 8mm MG	
	(one co-ax), two in hull	
Engine	V-8 105 hp SPA water-cooled, diesel	
Top speed	20 mph	
Range	125 miles	

The 47mm gun on the M13/40 had a better performance than the 37mm, however, it could

still only penetrate 23mm of armour at 1,500metres so its hitting power was well below that of its contemporaries - even the little British 2 pounder could penetrate 44mm whilst the American 37mm gun could penetrate 40mm at an equivalent range. Vehicles built towards the end of the production run did include desert modifications and were known as the M14/41, but they were actually much the same medium tank. A further development, the M15/42, which had a more powerful petrol engine plus a better 47mm gun, was designed in 1942, but only a few (about eighty) were actually built before production of this type ended in March 1943. Nevertheless, the M13 series was the backbone of Italian armoured forces. The Australians and British both made use of M 13/40s captured in early 1941

Instead of making more medium tanks, a series of self-propelled guns (*Semovente*) were produced being based on the M13, M14 and M15 tanks. A box-like superstructure was mounted on to the chassis with a mantlet in its front plate. The 75mm Ansaldo 75/18 howitzer, poked through this mantlet and had limited traverse (only 25 degrees each side). These guns were used as the main artillery support for Italian armoured divisions. In total 474 were built between 1941 and 1943.

Also produced in 1942, was the SP anti-tank gun *Semovente* M41. This mounted the Ansaldo 90/53 Model 39 anti-tank gun a powerful weapon, almost as powerful as the German 88mm. Unfortunately, it was almost too large to fit the M13/40 chassis, but was just squeezed onto the rear, with only a protective shield and no all-round protection for the gun crew. (In addition, only six rounds of ammunition could be carried on board). All of the thirty built were used in the defence of Sicily during the Allied invasion. In 1943, the even more powerful 105mm gun was mounted on the same chassis. Known as the 105/25 *Semovente* M42, a further thirty of these were built. Finally, just as the Germans had loaned the Italians twenty-four Panzers in 1943, they also loaned them twelve Stug IIIG.

The Italians were so impressed by the British Crusader that they decided to build a copy, with the same Christie-type suspension. The CA *Celere Sahariano*, was designed for desert fighting. The prototype was completed by early 1943 by which time the desert fighting was over and so the project was cancelled. Looking very much like Crusader, the tank mounted a 47mm gun although it was the intention to fit a 75mm to production models.

HEAVY TANKS

The CA P 26/40 was the only tank of any size or weight built during World War Two by the Italians and although they classified it as a heavy tank, it actually weighed only 26 tons. It owes its existence to Mussolini who gave orders, in 1940, for the tank to built. One was designed by Ansaldo and accepted in May 1942 followed by an order for 500 (later doubled). However, only twenty-one had been built before the surrender of Italy and these were commandeered by the Germans but saw little action.

Weight	26 tons	
Crew	four	
Dimensions	Length:	19ft 1in
	Width:	9ft 2ins
	Height:	8ft 3ins
Armour	14-50mm	
Armament	75mm plus MGs	
Engine	V-12 275hp diesel	
Top speed	22mph	

Although their engineers produced some interesting designs, Italy lacked the necessary heavy manufacturing industry, so their tanks were invariably inferior to contemporary Allied and German models.

CHAPTER EIGHT

Japan

'In the Japanese Army the tanks were dispersed amongst the infantry according to operational requirements, generally in small numbers, and did not undertake operations on their own account.'

'Tank Tracks to Rangoon' by Bryan Perrett

After World War One Japan showed an interest in tanks, obtaining a variety of models, such as the British Heavy Mk V and Medium A, also the ever-popular French Renault FT 17, which they named as KO-GATA Sensha (Sen – battle, Sha – wagon). In 1927, they purchased some Renault NC I (the successor to the FT 17) which they called OTSU-GATA Sensha. Both these sturdy little tanks were still in service in 1940. In 1922, they produced a 22-ton Experimental Heavy Tank No 1, which had a number of turrets and was presumably influenced by the Nbz/Char 2C/A1E1. Later, having purchased some of Vickers' export models (6 ton, Mk C and Carden-Loyd tankette) they began to develop their own light and medium tanks, some of which were used to good effect in Manchuria and Shanghai. In 1933, Major Tomio Hara designed a bellcrank scissors-type suspension, which had paired bogie wheels, (two pairs on each side,) connected by a single coil-spring mounted horizontally outside the hull. This type of suspension became a feature of many Japanese tanks for the next decade and as will be seen, they built plenty of different models. Four tank regiments were formed during 1933 to 1934 in Japan and Manchuria. By the time the Japanese started their war with China in 1937, they had a strong armoured force, comprising 1,060 tanks, with eight tank regiments in the field, however, many of these were tankettes or semi-obsolescent heavier models. Also, despite their success, the Japanese still did not see the tank as a battle winner.

Although they did form independent armoured units and advocated using tanks en masse, they in the main adopted the French system of small units, which seemed to work satisfactorily against the Chinese, who at the time had no proper anti-tank weapons. Japan continued to use its tanks like mobile pillboxes, paying little regard to tactical movement and seldom allowing them to operate independently. This eventually proved disastrous against both American armour in the Pacific and Commonwealth armour in the Far East. Japanese marines were also equipped with armour but, once the army ceased building amphibious tanks, development was taken over by the Navy.

In the period 1931-38, the Japanese had built nearly 1,700 tanks, which put them into fourth place in the world - behind only the Soviet Union, France and Germany. However, they decided to devote a major part of their heavy industry to the building of warships, AA weapons and aircraft principally because they still did not see the tank as a battle winner. Japan did continue to build tanks, even to increase output during 1940 and 1941, but after reaching peak annual production in 1942, the tank building industry declined and was unable to catch up once they realised their grave mistake by underestimating the abilities of the tank. Japanese manufacturers still produced some inovative designs, including a number of amphibious models, but by then it was a question of too little too late.

TANK PRODUCTION 1939-45

1939	-	345
1940	-	735
1941	-	1,190
1942	-	1,290
1943	-	780
1944	-	295
1945	-	130
Total 1939-45		4,765 *a*

Note: a. Added to the pre-war total this means that the Japanese built a total of 6,450 tanks. Of these, over half were constructed by Mitsubishi Heavy Industries Ltd:

Light tanks	-	1,200
Medium tanks	-	2,100
Amphibious tanks	-	300

(In addition Mitsubishi built fifty SP howitzers and 200 special purpose vehicles).

Japanese tanks were given names and designated by using the last two digits of the year in which production began. This they did by using the Japanese calendar, which begins at the year of foundation of their Empire, equivalent to 660 BC. To discover the year of production one must subtract 660. For example, the KE-NI light tank was known as the Type 98, being the last two digits of the year 2598, subtract 660 and one arrives at 1938. The war years 1939 to 1940 are: 2599 to

2605. To complicate matters, from the year 2600 (Western year 1940), they did try to simplify their system, by designating tanks in that year: Type 100 and so forth. This was followed by Type 1 for 2601, Type 2 for 2602.

Japanese tanks were classified as follows:

Up to 5 tons	- Tankettes	(Choki Sensha)
5 to 10 tons	- Light Tanks	(Ki Sensha)
10 to 20 tons	- Medium Tanks	(Chi Sensha)
Over 20 tons	- Heavy Tanks	(Ju Sensha)

TANKETTES

Like so many other nations in the interwar period, the Japanese bought several export models from Vickers, such as the Carden-Loyd Mk VI, then proceeded to copy it and develop their own tankettes. The first of these was the Type 94, a two-man 3.5 ton vehicle, which had armour 4 to 12mm thick and was armed with a single 7.7mm machine gun mounted in a small turret offset to the right. It was powered by a front-mounted 32hp petrol engine, which gave the 10ft long, 5ft 3ins wide and 5ft 4ins high vehicle, a top speed of 26mph and a range (estimated by US Intelligence) of 100 miles. The Type 94 was modified later, with a better suspension incorporating a trailing idler, which lengthened the chassis by about 12 inches, thus

Above: **The 3.5 ton Type-94 TK tankette was developed from the Vickers Carden-Loyd Mk VI, but with a small turret mounting a single 7.7mm machine gun.** *(TM)*

Above: **These tankettes, fording a stream in China, are towing light tracked trailers. A diesel version of the Type-94 TK was built but only as a prototype.** (TM)

increasing the length of track in contact with the ground and improving cross-country performance. Also there was some trials work carried out with diesel engines which produced a Type 94 diesel prototype, but this was later dropped. However, this work was of great value in developing an engine for the final tankette, the Type 97 TE-KE. This vehicle weighed over 4.5tons and was, at just over 12ft, two ft longer than the original Type 94.

A larger turret, mounting a 37mm gun was fitted but it still only only carried a crew of two. Power came from a rear-mounted 65hp diesel engine, allowing it a top speed of 28mph and a road range of 150 miles.

Some tankettes were used in forward areas as ammunition carriers and also as artillery OP vehicles. Large numbers were deployed to China for reconnaissance and other cavalry roles, and more saw service in most Pacific and Far East arenas during World War Two. Easily knocked out - because the armour was very thin – although an AP round might enter one side of the tankette and go out through the other without hitting a vital part! Nevertheless they were used with great dash and daring, but stood little chance against tanks such as the Sherman.

LIGHT TANKS

At the same time as building tankettes the Japanese decided to design larger, three-man vehicles to use for example, in supporting deep cavalry-type thrusts. Also they decided to develop amphibious vehicles, because of the lack of good roads, bridges and ferries which hampered movement in the Far

East. This development began between 1931 and 1932 with the Type 92 and an amphibious version of the same vehicle, the A-I-GO. The production version of the Type 92 was one of the earliest all-welded AFVs. The new running gear, which distinguishes it from its 1931 prototype, comprised six small rubber-tyred bogies, mounted in pairs, with three semi-elliptical springs. Later production models had this suspension replaced by four larger spoked wheels, grouped in pairs with helical coil springs and bell-cranks. Both models weighed 3.5 tons, had a crew of three, mounted one heavy 13mm MG in the hull and one ball-mounted light 6.5mm MG in a small turret. The 12ft 7ins long tank had armour only 6mm thick, was powered by a 45hp petrol engine and had a top speed of 21.6mph. Both models were produced in reasonable numbers and were still in active service during World War Two.

The A-I-GO had a watertight hull, which was enlarged to give more buoyancy also to allow the fitting of propellors and floats. Although it did not enter production, much useful information was gained from the design and this was used in the next amphibian, the SR-I or I-GO. This also did not progress further than the building of two pilots (one waterjet propelled with a speed of

5mph). After these two failures the army lost interest and further amphibious development was left to the Japanese navy.

The next light tank to be produced was the HA-G0, probably one of the two best Japanese tanks of World War Two - the other being the OTSU medium. In production from 1935 for seven years at Mitsubishi a total of 1,250 HA-GOs were built. The HA-GO had its turret (containing a 37mm gun in the front and a 7.7mm MG ball-mounted in the rear) offset to the left. The suspension was of Major Tomio Hara's design bellcrank and helical compression spring. The 7.5ton HA-GO was powered by a 110hp diesel engine. Developed later from the HA-GO was the KE-NI, which appeared in 1938, it had three pairs of bogie wheels instead of two, better armoured protection and was more streamlined than its predecessor. However, it was only produced in small numbers - approximately 200 built from 1942, apparently because the HA-GO was more popular with tank crews. There were two versions of the KE-NI, the Type 98-A and the Type 98-B. The latter had a completely different suspension system, modelled on the Christie fast tank- type with four large road wheels. The Type B however did not enter production.

Above: **Three British officers inspecting a Type-97 TE-KE tankette, bringing in to perspective the small size of the 4.7 ton vehicle.** *(TM)*

Far left: **The Type-97 TE-KE tankette entered service in 1938, mounted a 37mm gun and was built in greater numbers than any other Japanese tankette, but was obsolete by 1940-41.** *(TM)*

Above: **The Type-95 HA-GO was probably one of the best tanks built by the Japanese. Approximately 1,250 of this three-man, 7.5 ton-tank were built. Its main drawback was that the commander sat alone in the turret having to load, aim and fire the 37mm gun as well as command his tank.** *(TM)*

Specifications	Type 95 HA-GO	Type 98-A KE-NI
Weight (tons)	7.5	7.2
Crew	three	three
Dimensions		
Length:	14ft 4ins	13ft 6ins
Width:	6ft 9ins	6ft 11ins
Height:	7ft	6ft
Armour	6-12mm	6-16mm
Armament (both)	37mm gun	two 7.7mm MG
Engine	110hp diesel	150hp diesel
Top speed	25mph	31mph
Range	100miles	100miles

There were some further development models produced, the last being the KE-HO light tank Type 5, which had a crew of four was armed with a 47mm gun, and was powered by a 150hp supercharged diesel which gave the 10-ton tank a top speed of over 30mph. However, although it appears to have been an excellent machine the war ended before it entered production.

MEDIUM TANKS

The Japanese purchased a Vickers Mk C export model in 1927 and two years later developed, from it, their first medium tank the Type 89-KO (also called the Type 89-A), which retained many of the original features of the Vickers tank. A second model followed the Type 89-B (also called the Type 89 OTSU). The original Type 89 was petrol engined, but after cold weather trials in Man-

churia, it was decided to fit a diesel, the six-cylinder 115hp Mitsubishi engine developed especially for the tank. The Type 89 was widely used in China and Manchuria, where it was sometimes fitted with a unditching tail, as on the Renault FT 17. It continued in service up to 1943, being used also in the Pacific. However, its suspension was out-dated and clearly something better was needed.

Specifications	Type 89-KO	Type 89-OTSU
Weight (tons)	12.7	13
Crew	four	four
Dimensions		
Length:	19ft 3ins	19ft 3ins
Width:	7ft 1in	7ft 1in
Height:	8ft 6ins	8ft 6ins
Armour	10-17mm	10-17mm
Armament (both)	57mm two MG	(one in hull, one in rear of turret)
Engine	105hp petrol	115hp diesel
Top speed	15mph	15mph

In 1936, the Japanese launched a programme to find a successor to the Type 89, even though it had only just entered service. One design which won considerable praise was the CHI-NI, a 10-ton tank, with a top speed of 18.5mph and armed with a 57mm gun. Its rival the more expensive and heavier CHI-HA, was chosen for mass production and once war between Japan and China had begun, it was found that there was a need for a heavier, better protected tank. The CHI-HA performed well throughout World War Two but cannot really be compared with Allied medium tanks weighing only 15tons, with armour under 25mm thick.

Specifications	CHI-HA
Weight (tons)	15
Crew	four
Dimensions	
Length:	18ft 2ins
Width:	7ft 8ins
Height:	7ft 4ins
Armour	8-25mm
Armament	57mm short-barrelled gun, two MG (one in rear of turret, one in bow)
Engine	V-12 170hp diesel
Top speed	24mph
Range	130miles

The SHI-KI command version of the CHI-HA had an all-round aerial on the turret (in the style of early Soviet command tanks), and fitted a 37mm or 57mm gun in place of the bow MG, presumably because the turret guns were dummies. The SE-RI was the recovery version, which had a towing/lifting jib at the rear and a strange conical-shaped turret. It was powered by a 240hp diesel and weighed 15.5 tons. The mine clearing version was known simply as Type-G and was fitted with twin-flail drums (the idea copied from the Allies), whilst there was also a tank dozer with a front-mounted blade. Attempts were made to up-gun the CHI-HA, the short-barrelled 57mm being replaced by a high velocity 47mm long-barrelled gun. The resulting medium tank became known as SHINTO CHI-HA. Other attempts at improvement were as follows:

Left: **A Type-89 OTSU climbing a steep bank. The suspension, designed by Major Tomio Hara, was out-dated before 1939.** *(TM)*

Left: **Advancing across a damaged bridge is a 13 ton, four-man Type-89 OTSU, which still had many of the features of the British Vickers Medium C, from which it was developed.** *(TM)*

Medium tank Type-1 CHI-HE - armed with the new 47mm gun, redesigned superstructure, new turret and welded armour. Produced from 1941.

Gun tank Type-2 HO-I – similar to the CHI-HE, but with a 75mm short-barrelled gun, weight 16.5tons and five-man crew. Produced from 1942.

Medium tank Type-3 CHI-NU – as above but fitting a much larger turret with a 75mm Type 3 field gun, weight 18.5tons. Produced from 1943.

Medium tank Type-4 CHI-TO. – as above but with a longer chassis and a larger turret, mounting a 75mm Type 4 long-barrelled gun, developed from AA guns. Now weighing 30 tons. Did not enter production.

Medium tank Type-5 CHI-RI. – a 37ton tank with a massive turret, mounting a 75mm gun. Still at the development stage VJ-Day.

HEAVY TANKS

As explained, the Japanese first produced a heavy tank (the Experimental Tank No 1) at the Osaka Arsenal in 1927, then modified it in 1930. The first model weighed 20 tons, was multi-turreted and had a suspension system which comprised nineteen small bogie wheels on each side. In 1930 modifications were made to reduce its weight by 2 tons. This was achieved by thinning down the armour and reducing the number of bogie wheels to seventeen. At the same time the tank was up-gunned from 57 to 70mm. Both these experimental models were the forerunners of the Type-91 heavy tank (sometimes referred to as Type-92), and also multi-turreted. The Type-95 followed and was again multi-turreted, with a 37mm in the front sub-turret, a 70mm in the main turret plus a machine gun ball-mounted towards the rear. The rear turret mounted another MG. Only four were built, then the project was cancelled, although later some design work was carried out on a super heavy tank, mounting a 100mm gun.

Specifications	Type-91	Type-95
Weight (tons)	18	26
Crew	five	five
Dimensions		
Length:	21ft	21ft 6ins
Width:	8ft 3ins	9ft
Height:	8ft 8ins	9ft 8ins
Armour	up to 20mm	up to 30mm
Armament	70mm	70mm
	three MG	37mm
		two MG
Engine	240hp BMW	290hp BMW
	petrol	petrol
Top speed	15.5mph	13mph

AMPHIBIOUS TANKS

The Imperial Japanese Navy began producing amphibious tanks in 1942, the three main models being:

Type-2 KA-MI - the most successful and best known. This was a 9-ton tank, armed with a 37mm

gun and two MGs. For amphibious operations, two detatchable sponsons were fitted fore and aft being dropped once ashore. Propulsion in the water came from twin propellors, whilst steering was through two rudders. Total weight with sponsons and all waterproofing was 12.5tons.

Type-3 KA-CHI - larger and heavier, based on the CHE-HE medium tank, it weighed nearly 29 tons and also had detachable sponsons . It featured a circular chimney-type escape hatch surmounting the turret.

Type-5 TO-KU - the last to be designed, was slightly larger and heavier (just over 29 tons), but carried more firepower; a 47mm gun and MG in the front of the hull, with an MG and a naval-type 25mm cannon in the turret. It did not enter production.

CHAPTER NINE

Other Countries

Although tank production among the rest of the world was small, some good tanks were produced, especially those from Czechoslovakia which were then commandeered by Germany for the Panzerwaffe.

In addition to the major manufacturers of tanks in World War Two, a number of other countries did produce small numbers of tanks. Foremost of these was Czechoslovakia closely followed by neutral Sweden. The Czech tanks became an important part of the Panzerwaffe and played a major role in Blitzkriegs on both France and Russia. Swedish tanks did not see action, nevertheless they were well made and modern in design. Of the rest, the largest and best armed were Turans, built by Hungary.

CZECHOSLOVAKIA

When Germany annexed the country in March 1939 they took over the Czech Army's equipment and the armaments industry. Subsequently the Germans made considerable use of the tanks in service with the Czechoslovak Army - mainly the LT vz 35, designated by the Germans, PzKpfw 35(t) (t: *tchechoslowakisch* - Czech origin), which made up a large proportion of the Czech armoured forces at the time. Later they also used its successor, the LT vz 38 – known in German service as the PzKpfw 38(t), which was in 1939 only at the prototype stage. This was followed by Marder and Hetzer tank destroyers both of which used the 38(t) chassis, running gear and many other components.

Developed by Skoda in 1934-35, the LT vz 35 was an advanced tank design and incorporated many innovative features, which unfortunately led

to early development problems. However, these were mainly corrected before being commandeered by the Germans who used them successfully as gun tanks until 1941-42, then as turretless tractors. Combat weight was 10.5tons and it was armed with a 37mm Skoda A-3 gun. This had a distinctive armoured cowl, fitted over its recoil cylinder and protruded from the front of the turret. Alongside the main gun was a ball-mounted 7.92mm MG, which could be fired independently or coupled as a co-ax. A second MG was mounted in the hull, also in a ball-socket, to the left of the driver. Originally the crew was only three, but in German service this was sensibly increased to four (commander, gunner, loader/radio operator and driver). The hull and turret were of rivetted and bolted construction. Powered by a 120hp Skoda T11 water-cooled petrol engine, it was fitted with pneumatic transmission and steering to reduce driver fatigue. (In Russia this was a decided disadvantage, a special heater had to be fitted to prevent the steering system freezing solid). The suspension, which was good and reliable, had eight small bogies on each side, coupled in pairs and suspended on leaf springs. Tracklife was excellent – at least 5,000 miles.

The LT vz 35 originally entered service with the Czech Army in 1936, but by the end of the year all had been returned to the makers for defect repairs. Eventually in March 1939, of the 297 in service 218 were taken for use by German Panzer

divisions, the remaining seventy-nine for service with the Slovak 3rd Fast Division which fought in Russia. Many of those pressed into German service were used to equip the 6th Panzer Division - 'a fine reliable offspring of the Vickers 6-ton tank' is how one Panzer officer described the 35(t).

A few were converted into command tanks, by fitting extra radios and a collapsible frame aerial over the back deck. When replaced in front line service, some were converted to mortar tractors (*morserzugmittel*) or tractors (*zugkraftwagen*) which could carry 12 tons of stores. Both had a crew of two, no turret and a canvas cover over the open hull.

Specifications	PzKpfw 35(t)	PzKpfw 38(t) Ausf A
Weight (tons)	10.5	9.5
Crew	four	four
Dimensions		
Length:	16ft 1in	14ft 11ins
Width:	7ft	7ft
Height:	7ft 3ins	7ft 7ins
Armour	8-35mm	8-25mm
Armament	37mm gun	improved 37mm
	two MG	two MG
Engine	120hp Skoda T11	125hp Praga EPA
Top speed	25mph	25mph
Range	125miles	155miles

When the Czechs were re-equipping in the mid-1930s, they allocated large funds to find a replacement for the troublesome LT vz 35. There were six contenders - two from Skoda and four from Ceskomoravska Kolben Danek of Prague (CKD). The winner of the trial was the TNHP-S tank, which CKD had built for export. During over three months of exhaustive testing it logged 3,490 miles (including 958 miles on heavy terrain) without a single serious defect and only needed thirty minutes maintenance a day. It was accepted by the army and given the designation LT vz 38; an order for 150 was placed in July 1938, the first twenty due to be completed before the end of the year. However, the worsening international situation delayed production and eventually, the Germans took over the first nine tanks straight off the assembly line in May 1939!

It was immediately appreciated that the 38(t) was far superior to the German PzKpfw I and II, both in armour and firepower. The company CKD was now under German control, as Bohmisch Mahrische Maschinenfabrik (BMM) and was ordered to complete, rapidly, the first order for 150 and then to carry on and build a further 325. The initial model was the Ausf A, and was identical to the TNHP-S apart from carrying a fourth crewman at the expense of ammunition storage (eighteen rounds). The next production series Ausf B, C & D (325 built between January and November 1940) all had small modifications - such as the fitting of smoke grenade launchers on the rear. Between November 1940 and October 1941 a total of

Above: **The Hungarian-built Turan II, mounting a very good 75mm gun. Photographed probably in Russia, where the 1st Pancelos Hadosztaly (Hungarian Panzer Division) fought on the Don front, 1943.** *(TM)*

Right: **Best of the Czech-built tanks the TNHP-S. Designated LT vz 38 it was never used by their Army. Instead they were commandeered by the Germans and used (as the PzKpfw 38 (t)) to equip four Panzer divisions.** *(TM)*

Above: **The Germans seized 218, LT vz 35 light tanks from the Czech Army and designated them as PzKpfw 35(t).** *(TM)*

525 Ausf E & F were built by BMM. After the campaign in Poland, extra 25mm thick armour plates were added to all frontal surfaces and 15mm sheets of armour to the sides. The ninety tanks (Ausf S) originally destined for Sweden, were retained by the Germans for their own forces. The final version was the Ausf G, which had even more armour plates welded on increasing the weight up to nearly 9.5 tons. Not all chassis were used for tanks, some being completed as SP anti-tank guns. In total 1,414 (including three prototypes) PzKpfw 38(t) were produced.

Final development came in 1942, with the manufacture of a small number of PzKpfw 38(t) neuer Art. These tanks were similar to the 38(t) but had 35mm thick welded armour and a new V-8 Praga engine, which gave the tank (now weighing almost 15 tons), a top speed of nearly 40mph. The neuer Art did not enter production.

The British had tested a TNHP in February 1939, but did not show much interest, despite the fact that it was superior to all British light tanks and compared favourably with the A9. The Germans nevertheless fully appreciated their true value, indeed without TNHP they would have had four less Panzer divisions for Operation Barbarossa.

Two tank destroyers (*Panzerjaeger*) were based on the 38(t) chassis, the first being the Marder III, which mounted a captured Russian 7.62cm field gun. Various other anti-tank guns were later used, including the 7.5cm Pak 40/3. The second type Hetzer, used the well-proven 38(t) components in a new low profile design, with 60mm of frontal armour and a 75mm Pak 39 gun. A total of 2,854 of both types were built up to March 1945. A number of variants of 38(t) Hetzer included a recovery vehicle (*Bergepanzer*) a flamethrower (*Flammpanzer*), ammunition carrier, SP and AA guns. There was also a driver training vehicle which, was fuelled by a wood-burning gas generator.

POLAND

Although Poland had only limited industrial capacity, it still took an active interest in armoured warfare and tank design. Sadly, most of the promising tanks had not reached production before the Germans invaded on 1 September 1939. The Army was only equipped with a mixture of obsolescent tankettes and light tanks, plus various foreign tanks purchased in the 1930s. Figures vary as to the exact strength of the Polish armoured forces at the outbreak of war, however, it would appear that under 1,000 light tanks and

Below: **The 1930 TK-3 was an improved version of the TK-1 and TK-2 tankettes, 300 being built. It weighed only 2.4 tons.** (TM)

tankettes were available to face the 3,000 plus tanks of the Panzerwaffe.

Polish armour was organised into separate battalions and independent companies, mainly spread among the infantry divisions. There was one all-arms mechanised brigade (10th Cavalry, known as the 'Black Brigade' because of their unique black leather coats), commanded by Colonel Stanislaw Macek, who would become a tank hero in the mould of Guderian and Rommel. The entire Polish tank force comprised approximately: 400-500 TK and TKS tankettes; 150-170, 7-TP light tanks; 50 Vickers 6-ton light tanks; 50 Renault R 35 light tanks and 50 Renault FT 17 light tanks

The first Polish tankette TK 1, was developed in 1929 and based on the British Vickers Carden-Loyd Mk VI, it weighed 1.75 tons and was armed with a single machine gun. It was followed into service by the TK 2. Serious production did not begin until 1931, with the TK 3 - an improved version of the TK 1 and TK 2 with an enclosed superstructure, a total of 300 were built. In 1931, a small four-wheeled trailer was designed to be towed behind the TK 3. However, this was not for carrying stores but to carry the tankette itself on long road journeys. The tankette was driven onto the trailer, its tracks removed and a chain-drive used to connect the tank's driving sprockets to the trailer's rear axle! Between 1936 and 1939, some development work was carried out to up-gun the TK 3 by mounting a 20mm automatic cannon in a large ball mount.

The TKS, developed in 1933, was an improved version of the TK, with armour now up to a maximum thickness of 10mm. A production order for 390 was placed, and work started in early

1934, a small number being built with cast armour. Further development of the TKS included the TKW (fully traversing turret), TKS-D (37mm Bofors anti-tank gun in an exposed position on top of the chassis, with just a reinforced front plate) and TKF (uprated range,

Above: **The TKW tankette was produced in 1934, with a fully traversing turret.** (TM)

46hp Fiat engine and a combination gun mount with one heavy and one light MG), none of which entered full production.

Specifications		TK3	TKS
Weight (tons)		2.4	2.6
Crew		two	two
Dimensions	Length:	8ft 6ins	8ft 5ins
	Width:	5ft 10ins	5ft 9ins
	Height:	4ft 4ins	4ft 5ins
Armour		3-8mm	3-10mm
Armament		MG	MG
Engine		40hp Ford petrol	46hp Fiat petrol
Top speed		28.5mph	25mph

The 7-TP was the Polish version of the Vickers 6 ton (twin turrets), but with thicker armour (up to 17mm) which increased combat weight up to nearly 9.5tons. The three-man light tank was powered by a 110hp Saurer diesel engine (the world's first diesel-powered tank) which gave it a top speed of 20mph. It was armed with two machine guns and was 15ft 1in long, 7ft 11ins wide and 7ft high. In 1937, a revised model went into production, this had a single turret which mounted a 37mm Bofors anti-tank gun and a co-ax MG with armour now increased to 15mm thick. The final model was the 7-TP (Improved), which had a much roomier turret with a rear bustle, thicker welded armour (up to 40mm), better suspension and wider tracks. All the improvements increased combat weight up to just over 11tons.

Other tanks under development at the outbreak of war included:

Small tank 4-TP - 4.3ton, two-man reconnaissance tank designed in 1936, with a turret offset to left. Only one prototype built, also based on the same chassis was an amphibious tank which never entered production.

Wheel & Track fast tank 10-TP - weighed 12.8tons, had Christie-type suspension, was fitted with a V-12 210hp engine, had 20mm thick armour and a 37mm gun. On test at the outbreak of war.

Medium tank 14-TP - similar to 10-TP, the weight increased to 14 tons and was powered by a 300hp Maybach engine. The uncompleted prototype was destroyed..

Heavy tank 20/25-TP - a multi-turret design considered in 1936, but never built.

HUNGARY

Prior to World War Two, Hungary had equipped its armoured forces with AFVs from abroad (Italian CV-33 tankettes) which they then modified to suit their own purposes. Nicholas Straussler, best known for his work on amphibious vehicles, produced some light tank designs before emigrating to Britain.

In 1940, Hungary gained permission to manufacture a medium tank which appeared in 1941 and was based on a Czech Skoda design. But again, like their pre-war AFVs, they adapted it for their purposes. Named Turan I, it was a 16-ton medium tank with a five-man crew and mounted a 40mm Skoda gun in a large rivetted turret (with square cupola). Turan was built by the Weiss & Cspel Steelworks of Budapest and was powered by 260hp Hungarian made engine. Further models included: Turan II - modified turret with long bevel on the cupola and the

gun changed to a short-barrelled 75mm; Turan III – as II, but now armed with a long-barrelled 75mm with muzzle brake; and the Zrinyi SP – 105mm howitzer on Turan chassis.

SWEDEN

Neutral Sweden started taking an interest in tank design when Joseph Vollmer, the designer of Germany's only tank to see service in World War One – the cumbersome A7V – slipped into Sweden in 1919, bringing with him ten 'kits' of his latest light tank (*Leichter Kampfwagen II*). These he sold to the interested Swedes, who used them (now designated Strv m/21) to equip their first tank unit. Vollmer then moved on to Czechoslovakia where he became chief designer for the Adamov company – the Germans would reap the rewards of his labours when they took over the Czech tank industry.

Little further progress was made in Sweden until the late 1920s when Germany began to covertly re-arm. The country then became a safe haven for firms like the giant Krupps, which was able to set up a company in Sweden. Their factory Landswerk AB at Landskrona soon began producing a series of advanced designs for both tanks and armoured cars – several of which incorporated new features. These features would find their way to Germany and the Soviet Union, who were at the time collaborating at the secret tank testing centre of Kazan. The 'Father of the Panzerwaffe', Heinz Guderian, drove his first tank (one of Vollmer's!) in Sweden which appeared in 1934, .

One of their best designs of this period was the

Strv L-60 light tank. It weighed just under 7 tons, mounted a 20mm cannon. It would be progressively improved with better armament, eventually being developed into the Strv m/40.

When war began, the two standard tanks of the Swedish army were Strv m/37 (a 4.5 tons light tank of Czech design built under licence in Sweden) armed with twin MGs and Strv m/38 8.5 ton, developed from the L60 and armed with a 37mm gun. Further development of this series included the Strv m/39, Strv m/40 and Strv m/40K.

Specifications	m/37	m/38	m/40K	m/42
Weight (tons)	4.5	8.5	11	22.5
Crew	two	three	three	four
Armour (max)	15mm	13mm	24mm	80mm
Armament	two MG	37mm	37mm	75mm
		one MG	two MG	three MG
Engine	80hp	142hp	160hp	410hp
	Volvo		Scania Vabis	
Top speed	30mph	28mph	28mph	30mph

Additionally in 1938, the Swedes had felt that they had a shortage of tanks, and placed an order with the Czechs for the TNHSv built by CKD. Although the Swedish order was appropriated by Germany, the Swedes had fortunately obtained permission to build TNHSv under licence. The new tank was designated Strv m/41 and over 200 were manufactured by Scania Vabis. The last tank produced by Sweden during World War Two, Strv m/42 was designed by Landsverk AB, weighed 26 tons and mounted a 75mm gun. The Strv m/42 was an excellent tank in all respects and would carry on in service after the war had ended.

Above: **The Swedish Strv m/40 K was the late production model of the m/40 and incorporated heavier armour increasing overall weight to almost 11 tons. Swedish-built tanks were not used in battle during World War Two.** *(TM)*

Index

Reference to photographs shown in *italics*

Turan	199, 202		Type 95 light tank	193, 194
			Type 96 medium tank	195
Tanks (Japan)			Type 97 medium tank	195, 196
Type 1 medium tank	196		Type 97 tankette	193
Type 2 amphibious tank	197		Type 98 light tank	**193**
Type 2 medium tank	196			
Type 3 amphibious tank	197		**Vickers Carden-Loyd**	
Type 3 medium tank	196, 197		tankette	56, 66, 158, 182,
Type 4 medium tank	196, 197			190, 191, 201
Type 5 amphibious tank	197		**Vickers Light Tank**	15, 33, 159, 201,
Type 5 light tank	194			202
Type 5 medium tank	196		**Vickers Medium Tank**	9, 19, 33, 56, 120
Type 89 medium tank	193, 194, 195			
Type 91 heavy tank	196		**Whippet**	8
Type 92 light tank	193			
Type 94 tankette	191, 192		**Zrinyi SP**	203
Type 95 heavy tank	196			

Some tanks acquired a huge variety of names during their careers – a different name might have been bestowed on one model by the manufacturer, the military authority, the crews and the enemy. The following guide may be of some help.

A9	Medium Cruiser Mk I		ATO	T-34/76
A10	Medium Cruiser Mk II		Australian Cruiser	Sentinel
A11/12 Matilda	Infantry Tank Mk I and II		*Bataillonführerswagen*	PzKpfw IV
A13	Medium Cruiser Mk IV,V		*Befelswagen*	PzKpfw
A15	Medium Cruiser Mk VI		Bergepanther	PzKpfw V
A17	Light Tank Mk VII		Black Prince	Infantry Tank A43
A20 (GB)	Infantry Tank A20		*Brummbär*	PzKpfw IV
A22 Churchill	Infantry Tank MkIV		1/BW	PzKpfw IV
A24	Medium Cruiser Mk VII		CA light tank	M11/39
A25	Light Tank Mk VIII		Carden-Loyd	Vickers Carden-Lloyd
A27L Centaur	Medium Cruiser Mk VIII		Cavalier	Medium Cruiser Mk VII
A27M Cromwell	Medium Cruiser Mk VIII		*Celere Sahariano*	CA *Celere Sahariano*
A30 (GB)	Medium Cruiser A30		Centaur	Medium Cruiser Mk VIII (A27L)
A-30 (Russian)	T-32		Centurion	Heavy Cruiser A41
A33	Cromwell		Chaffee	Infantry Light Tank M24
A34	Medium Cruiser A34		*Char de Rupture*	Char 2C
A38 Valiant	Infantry Tank A38		CHE-HE	Type 3
A39	Tortoise		CHI-HA	Type 97
A41	Centurion Heavy Cruiser		CHI-HE	Type 1
A43 Black Prince	Infantry Tank A43		CHI-NI	Type 96
ACGI	AMC		CHI-NU	Type 3
A-I-GO	Type 92		CHI-RI	Type 5
AMR-VM	AMR33		CHI-TO	Type 4
AMR-Z2	AMR35		Christie Convertible	M1931
AT26	T-26		Churchill	Infantry Tank MkIV
			Covenanter	Medium Cruiser Mk V
			Cromwell Cruiser	Medium Cruiser Mk VIII (A27M)
			Cruiser	Medium Cruiser
			Crusader	Medium Cruiser Mk VI

Durchbruchswagen	PzKpfw	Panther	PzKpfw V
		PanzerKampfwagen	PzKpfw
Elephant	PzKpfw Vl	Pershing	Heavy Tank M26
FCM36	Char Léger	PR	Light Tank Mk Vll
	FCM36	Purdah	Light Tank Mk Vll
Ferdinand	PzKpfw Vl	PzKpfw 35R	Char Léger R35
Fiat-Ansaldo L3	CV-33	PzKpfw 35-S	S35
Firefly	Medium Tank M4	PzKpfw 38H	H35, H39
		PzKpfw B2	Char B
General Grant	Medium Tank M3		
General Lee	Medium Tank M3	R35	Char Léger R35
Gorilla (M41 HMC)	Light Tank M24	R40	Char Léger R40
		Renault	AMC, Char Léger
H40	H39		R35, AMR35, R40
HA-GO	Type 95		
Harry Hopkins	Light Tank Mk Vlll	*Schnellkampfwagen*	PzKpfw ll
Hetzer	PzKpfw 38 (t)	SdKfz	PzKpfw 1
HO-I	Type 2	*Semovente M42*	M15/42
Honey	Infantry Light Tank	SE-RI	Type 97
	M3	SHI-KI	Type 97
Hotchkiss	H35, H39, H40	SHINTO CHI-HA	Type 97
Hummel	PzKpfw lV	Skink	Grizzly
		Sherman	Medium Tank M4
I-GO	Type 92	Somua	S35, S40
Infantry Light Tank (US)		SR-I	Type 92
– M19	M24	Stuart	Infantry Light Tank
– M41	M24		M3
– T7	Medium Tank M7	StuG	PzKpfw
– T9	M22	*SturmGeschutz*	PzKpfw
– T24	M24	*Sturmpanzer*	PzKpfw lV
IS	KV-IS	Super Churchill	Infantry Tank A43
IT-28	T-28	*Tauchpanzer*	PzKpfw lV
		TE-KE	Type 94, 97
Jagdpanther	PzKpfw V	Tetrach	Light Tank Mk Vll
		Tiger	PzKpfw Vl
KA-CHI	Type 3	TNHP	PzKpfw 38 (t)
	amphibious tank	TO-KU	Type 5
KA-MI	Type 2		amphibious tank
	amphibious tank	Type 92	Type 91 heavy tank
KE-HO	Type 5		
	amphibious tank	Valentine	Infantry Tank Mklll
KE-NI	Type 98 light tank	Valiant	Infantry Tank A38
Kleiner panzer befelswagen	PzKpfw	VK601	PzKpfw I
Ko-gata Sensha	Renault FT17	VK901	PzKpfw lll
Königstiger	PzKpfw V	VK903	PzKpfw lll
L35	CV-33	VK1301	PzKpfw lll
Locust	Infantry Light Tank	VK1601	PzKpfw lll
	M22	VK1801	PzKpfw 1
LT vz 35	PzKpfw 35 (t)	VK2001	PzKpfw lV
LT vz 38	PzKpfw 38 (t)	VK3001	PzKpfw Vl
Luchs	PzKpfw lllz	VK3002	PzKpfw Vl
		VK3601	PzKpfw Vl
Marder	PzKpfw 38 (t)	VK4501	PzKpfw Vl
Matilda	Infantry Tank	VK6501	PzKpfw Vl
	Mk l and Mk ll		
Nbz	PzKpfw Vl		
NC1 and 2	Char NC1 and 2	*Zugführerwagen*	PzKpfw lll
NC27	Char NC1	ZW	PzKpfw lll
NC31	Char NC2		
Neubaufahrzeug	PzKpfw Vl		
OT	T-26		
OTSU	Type 89		
OTSU-GATA SENCHA	Renault NC1		

Fitters at work changing a drive-sprocket on a PzKpfw VI Ausf E, Tiger. (GF)